Praise for
Selling Water by the River

"The unique thing I've seen Shane do time and time again is take a truth with all of its complexity and edges and implications and capture it in a metaphor...It's really, really profound and really helpful and really inspiring. This book is no exception: It's packed full of these tight little stories and examples and images and pictures that you'll be turning over in your mind and heart long after you've closed the book."   —Rob Bell, author of *Love Wins*

"There are, in Hipps's SELLING, a sturdiness and brilliance and simplicity of theology and an accessible and God-drenched grace that make it the humblest, clearest, most comfortably compelling statement yet of the difference between 'religious Christianity' and the Jesus way. In sum, this is one of the most instructive and pastoral books I have read in the last ten years and, Lord knows, one of the most needed."

—Phyllis Tickle, lecturer on religion in America and author of *Emergence Christianity: What It Is, Where It Is Going, and Why It Matters*

"Shane Hipps brings us news that is too good not to be true: that what we thought we had to wait for, work for, strive for, reach for, fight for, die for, earn, learn, master, or attain is actually already a gift fully given in the present of this moment, graciously and freely ours if only we would awaken to it. This book not only offers us this good news with great clarity and delight; it also helps us—gently, wisely, simply, and profoundly—to be roused and raised into that blessed state of awe and awakening."

—Brian D. McLaren, author of *Why Did Jesus, Moses, the Buddha, and Mohammed Cross the Road?* (www.brianmclaren.net)

"Masterfully weaving story, metaphor, and scripture into a tapestry, Shane Hipps puts his finger on something we all long for: a connection with the Divine. SELLING WATER BY THE RIVER will be a wonderful discovery for the many people who feel that true spirituality has been corrupted by culture and religion."

—Tony Jones (tonyj.net), theologian and author of many books, including *The New Christians*

"This book is one of the flare-ups from that religionless Christianity that more and more is breaking out in our world. Some of us will flee from what Shane Hipps tries to tell us in this book. Others will find what he has to say helpful in their efforts to live out the Jesus lifestyle in the landscape of a post-modern world. Whatever your reactions might be you will find the words on these pages cannot be ignored."

—Tony Campolo, Eastern University

"Shane Hipps manages to take your beliefs and assumptions about God and the Bible and artfully, yet mercilessly wrings them out, leaving behind whatever drips to the floor, (the things that never belonged in there anyhow), then shakes them out and shows them to you again now free from what had clung to them—and before you is something beautiful, true, new and familiar."

—Nadia Bolz-Weber, founding pastor,
House for all Sinners and Saints

Also by Shane Hipps

Flickering Pixels:
How Technology Shapes Your Faith

The Hidden Power of Electronic Culture:
How Media Shapes Faith, the Gospel, and Church

Selling Water by the River

■ ■ ■

A BOOK ABOUT THE LIFE
JESUS PROMISED AND THE RELIGION
THAT GETS IN THE WAY

SHANE HIPPS

JERICHO
BOOKS

New York   Boston   Nashville

Jericho Books
Hachette Book Group
237 Park Avenue
New York, NY 10017
www.JerichoBooks.com

Printed in the United States of America

RRD-C

First edition: October 2012
10 9 8 7 6 5 4 3 2 1

Jericho Books is a division of Hachette Book Group, Inc.
The Jericho Books name and logo are trademarks of Hachette Book Group, Inc.

The Hachette Speakers Bureau provides a wide range of authors for speaking events. To find out more, go to www.HachetteSpeakersBureau.com or call (866) 376-6591.

The publisher is not responsible for websites (or their content) that are not owned by the publisher.

Library of Congress Cataloging-in-Publication Data

Hipps, Shane, 1956–
    Selling water by the river : a book about the life Jesus promised and the religion that gets in the way / Shane Hipps. — 1st ed.
      p. cm.
    ISBN 978-1-4555-2208-8
    1. Jesus Christ—Buddhist interpretations.   I. Title.
    BT304.914.H57 2012
    232—dc23

                                                              2012021162

For my teacher,
the muse,
and Harper and Hadley

CONTENTS

DUST FROM STRINGS

Our Most Basic Quest

The desire begins with the first breath.

The moment life first dances in the body, a longing is born in the human heart.

A desire so simple and powerful that it drives a singular quest. This longing is baked into our being whether we want it or not. The longing is as innate to us as our thirst for water.

The object of our thirst goes by many names. Some call it love, others peace, others still joy or happiness. The list goes on. Regardless of the name we give it, the reality it points to is the same.

We search for it in all we do. We arrange nearly everything in our lives to quench that thirst. We look for it in our family and friends, in work and rest, in sex and marriage, in exercise and ice cream.

Some of us will look for it in the renunciation of these very things.

The objects of these pursuits present one problem. Whatever feeling they evoke, whatever thirst they quench, whatever joy they create, it never seems to last. Eventually, our husband's gaze returns to his favorite glowing screen, our wife becomes cold and critical, our body fails us, the pay doesn't match the hours, the sex ends, a loved one leaves, children act out, the bowl of ice cream is empty, and the buzz wears off.

Soon the hunger returns and the quest begins again.

The problem is not the pursuit of these things. They are meant to be enjoyed. The problem is the nature of these things. They are temporary, and therefore so is their effect.

Our joy will share the fate of the thing we bind it to.

And here we arrive at the central problem of this life—it doesn't last.

Everyone and everything, everywhere eventually returns to the dust.

The slightest awareness of such an inconvenient fact charges our quest with even more urgency. We become bent on pursuing a peace that is permanent, unchanging, and eternal. A joy that is not susceptible to the weather, and stays with us beyond the grave.

This is where religion comes in. Every religion promises a solution to the problem of death and the crisis of meaning. Every religion claims to be the sole portal to that permanent peace or the pathway to life after death. Each offers scripture and teachers, doctrines and dogmas, rules and regulations, rituals and practices, music and architecture, all intended to give access to that lasting peace.

You can find members of that religion who will defend it, sometimes to the death (either their own or someone else's). You can also find those disillusioned by that same religion who vehemently denounce it; it failed them, injured them, betrayed them, or let them down.

Today we have more religions than at any other time in human history, and more variations on those religions than ever before. Each variation offers a new razor-thin distinction, driven by the need to correct the failings of a previous iteration.

I am a Christian, and have been for twenty-five years. I've been a church leader for a decade. In these years of practicing and serving as a religious leader, I have come to believe that a big difference exists between the power and purpose of Jesus and the religion that bears his name. Christianity is a powerful aid to billions of people. While its history is riddled with abuses and dark deeds, on balance, I believe the world is better with it. This view is colored by the countless lives I have seen transformed because of it—my own included.

However, we must be careful not to confuse Christ with Christianity.

One is the river; the other sells water by the river. Christ is the river; the Christian religion attempts to package and provide access to water that is readily available to anyone at any time.

Often the merchant gets in the way of the water it wants to provide. Ironically, the religion that proclaims Jesus sometimes builds the biggest barriers to him.

By using the words "selling" and "merchant" I am not referring to the "prosperity gospel" or any other particular expression of Christianity. I am referring to Christianity as a whole, which serves as a gatekeeper for something that does not have or even need a gate.

My interest, however, is not in getting rid of the merchant. To do so would be like trying to get rid of the clouds in the sky. I am hardly a defender of religion, but this does not mean I am opposed to it. I recognize its value. For this reason, I do not advocate that we somehow become more *spiritual but not religious*. After all, Jesus was very religious by most standards, and he never once talked about "spirituality."

Instead, my interest is in the water—the experience of deep joy, boundless love, and indestructible peace that Jesus promised. I want to remind us that the river was here before the merchant. The river is available with or without the merchant, it is here despite the current failings of the merchant, and it will be here long after this merchant is gone. While this river does not resist an intermediary, it doesn't need one either.

This river gives water to all who are thirsty.

The reason this river doesn't need an intermediary is simple. As I intend to show in the pages that follow, Jesus tells us the river is already flowing within us right now. According to Jesus, nothing stands between it and us. The most overlooked aspect of the Good News is that we already have what we are looking for, and Jesus came to show us how to experience it.

The eternal life Jesus promised isn't just

something we must wait for until we die, and we don't have to go searching for it on the top of some mountain, or in the renunciation of possessions, or in the pursuit of justice, or in the profession of certain beliefs and the denunciation of others. These methods are the currency of the merchant—religion. Nothing is wrong with them, but they are not requirements of the river. The river is only interested in our thirst and trust in the One who guides us to it.

It is possible to arrive at this conclusion through philosophical reasoning, biblical interpretation, and theological argument. However, such a conclusion would not mean very much. We must taste this water, not merely believe in it. It is an experience of the heart, not a thought in the mind.

While I will make use of these intellectual techniques in this book, my view is born first of a deeply personal encounter—an encounter not easily reduced to words. As a result, I write about it only briefly here.

I have had many moments, often in the darkest hours of my life, where something remarkable happened. A radiant joy at the center of my being opened like a rose, an overwhelming peace and bright bliss burned through my sorrow like a lamp in my chest.

This experience has persisted many times regardless of the ups or downs of my life circumstances. Over time, these experiences have caused me to see the words of Jesus in an entirely new light. This experience of quenching a deep thirst from the inside is not unique to me; others know it too, and I believe it is a possibility for anyone who wants it.

I don't always live there. I am tossed about as much as the next person, but because of these experiences I have come to realize that the river is real and I know someone who can lead me to it. Each day I get a little better at trusting it and choosing moment by moment to find my way to that Living Water where I can drink my fill.

I am convinced that this is the life Jesus promised—the experience of peace, joy, and love while we live, not just after we die.

The world presents us with countless obstacles to Jesus and the life he promised. We are often and easily distracted from the river on the inside by the promise of things on the outside—our work, wealth, or relationships. When these things are going well, we don't need the river, and when they are going badly, we become so focused on fixing our problems that we forget about the river. Equally problematic are the beliefs that we are taught to adopt that truncate our imagination of God and limit us. They can prevent us from accepting the gift God offers. Then there is the issue of fear. Fear is one of the great barriers to this river. It profoundly distorts our ability to see the gift as it really is.

Ironically, religious Christianity is often the purveyor of the very beliefs and fears that get in the way of the water.

Beliefs are an important part of any religion. What we believe matters, but not for the reasons we may assume. Our beliefs (or lack of beliefs) do not qualify or disqualify us from the river. Instead, they determine how clearly we will see the river, which is always running just beneath our noses. Some beliefs clear the way and give us high visibility, while others create a thick fog. The distance between the river and us never actually changes. What changes is how well we can see and accept it.

I am convinced that many of the barriers to the water created by religious Christianity share a common source—the ways we have been told to under-stand and interpret the Bible.

The Bible contains sixty-six books, in dozens of literary genres, written by nearly as many authors, in multiple languages, over several thousand years. The Bible is not merely a book, but an extensive library capable of conveying wide and brilliant truths. The Bible is like a piano with a vast range of notes and capable of playing an endless array of songs.

In the last few centuries, Christian institutions have narrowed the range of notes it plays, resulting in a simple song easily learned and repeated. But through time, repetition makes any song, no matter how beautiful, lose its edge and interest.

The fresh becomes familiar and what was once powerful becomes predictable. Familiarity breeds predictability, and this leads to boredom.

Today, we are in danger of believing that nothing new can come from the pages of this ancient book.

But the notes that have been neglected are wait-ing to resound with songs that still surprise. Strings long silent are now eager to sing. This book is an effort to let sound these neglected notes, to strike the dust from those strings and let a new song rise.

A song big enough for a complex world.

A song that wakes the weary from their boredom and sleep.

A song resounding with the boundless, brilliant, and indestructible love of God.

BENDING LIGHT

The Lenses We Look Through

The new eyeglasses made my eighth-grade face moony and bookish. Adolescent insecurity said, *There's no way I need glasses. I can see just fine.* That conviction disappeared the moment I donned my new frames. It's a strange experience getting glasses for the first time. Before, trees from a distance were just puffy green clouds hovering over trunks. Glasses on: All of a sudden trees had leaves, objects had definition. The world changed instantly. Apart from my terribly unfortunate new look, this was quite thrilling.

A few years before that, the term "learning disability" was applied to my particular style of learning, or not learning. A handful of specialists were busy diagnosing and offering different treatments.

During one of my many assessments, a specialist had me read a paragraph out loud from a book, and would overlay different colored transparency sheets on top as I read—blue, brown, orange, green, red, and so on. With each new sheet I was to continue reading while she noted any changes.

What she found is that when viewed through the blue tinted sheet, my reading would speed up and smooth out. From my perspective, colors like red and orange made the horizontal lines of text on the page practically vanish, leaving a sea of scrambled letters. Once the blue sheet was placed over the page, the horizontal lines would snap back in full relief.

It turns out that certain frequencies of light were causing my eye problems. The blue screen blocked the necessary frequencies, whereas the red and orange only amplified the wrong ones. It didn't fix all the problems, but it helped. Eventually I was given *blue*-tinted glasses to help my reading—yay. (Needless to say, I wore them only in private. I have my dignity.)

A lens is a simple technology. It either bends or blocks light. That's it.

But lenses have another interesting feature. When working properly, a lens is invisible. It is not something we see, but something we see *through*. And it determines the way we see, what we see, and what we don't.

No one comes to the Bible or life without a lens. Our lenses are mostly invisible to us, but they determine how we understand the Bible and the world around us.

A lens can be a set of assumptions or beliefs that we have. Sometimes it can be an emotion like fear or anger. When it comes to the Bible, religious authorities usually tell us which lenses we should use. We learn what to believe about the Bible as a way to help us understand how to read it. We are also taught what to be afraid of or angry about. And our unique "prescription" is comprised of multiple assumptions like the stacked lenses the eye doctor uses, each one bending or blocking light to help us see more clearly—or in some cases, less clearly.

My first set of biblical lenses was given to me in college. Lens #1: The Bible is the Word of God. Lens #2: The Bible is flat; no teaching or doctrine in the Bible is privileged above another. Lens #3: The Bible has no errors, historically, scientifically, or grammatically. Lens #4: The Bible is unified in its message. Lens #5: God doesn't speak outside the Bible.

This is how I was taught to see the Bible. This set of lenses was given to me by authority figures I trusted and liked, so I assumed they were accurate. They were smarter than me and had done a lot more study on the subject. In time and through study, I learned something fascinating—some of these lenses are drawn from the Bible itself, but others are simply assumptions born of reason, theology, religion, tradition, experience, or observation. They were not infallible and were often chosen unconsciously. This understanding changed what I saw.

Authority figures also told me about other lenses that I shouldn't look through, as they were dangerous and could distort my vision. Things like:

1. The Bible is a collection of ancient literary works, like an archeological artifact.

2. Some parts of the Bible should be read metaphorically, not literally.

3. The Bible is a human document attempting to describe the Divine.

4. The Bible contains many diverse messages.

5. The Bible is just the first word. Not the final word.

While I appreciated their warnings, when I rebelled and tried some of these lenses on I started to see Jesus and faith in new, liberating depth. These and other lenses no longer scared me. They allowed me to explore more deeply, like turning a diamond to see its many facets. Some angles were more interesting, helpful, and revealing than others.

Our lenses—our assumptions, our way of seeing the world—shape the way we interpret the Bible and how we relate to God and those in the world around us.

When we see our lenses, we can evaluate them consciously. We can even begin to make decisions about them. We may encounter the limits of our lenses. Do they need to be cleaned? Do they distort too much? Do they need to be repaired or replaced? What would happen if we experimented with a different lens? Are there other lenses that may help us see something new, different, even better?

When I got glasses, the world didn't change, only the way I saw it. I saw things more clearly. An examination of our lenses is not a process of changing the Bible, the world, or truth; it is a process of changing ourselves.

The most limited Bible interpreter is one who claims to have no lens.

Even Jesus, the son of God, made deliberate use of a lens.

In Matthew 22:34–40, Jesus is talking with a group of very religious people: the Pharisees. They ask him a trick question.

> Hearing that Jesus had silenced the Sadducees, the Pharisees got together. One of them, an expert in the law, tested him with this question: "Teacher, which is the greatest commandment in the Law?"
>
> Jesus replied: "'Love the Lord your God with all your heart and with all your soul and with all your mind.' This is the first and greatest commandment. And the second is like it: 'Love your neighbor as yourself.' All the Law and the Prophets hang on these two commandments."

The story says that the Pharisees were trying to test Jesus. Why is this a test? Because the only proper way to answer it is to say that every commandment is the greatest. God did not issue 613 "suggestions" or "ideas for living." They were called "commandments" for a reason. They are meant to be taken seriously. So the only "correct" way to answer the question is to say that all the commandments are the greatest.

But that is not how Jesus answers. He says that some commandments are more important than others. Some commandments are primary and others are secondary. All of the law and the prophets are to be interpreted through the two greatest commandments, which are to love God and love your neighbor as yourself. These are the most important. The others are to be understood in light of these two.

The implications of what Jesus says here are enormous and often overlooked. He is actually showing us that he has a lens—a set of assumptions. He doesn't see the Bible as flat: it has peaks and valleys, some parts that matter more than other parts. That doesn't mean that the lesser ones are invalid; they just carry less weight.

In a Roman arch, all the stones depend upon one stone at the top called the keystone. It is shaped differently than the others, and it's the most important stone in the construction. Without the keystone there is no arch, only a pile of blocks on the ground. Jesus teaches that certain parts of God's Word carry a kind of keystone authority.

Love God and love your neighbor as yourself: these two form the keystone. Everything else in the Bible is secondary to these two commandments. It doesn't mean that all we need is a keystone, but rather that this single stone holds the whole structure together.

This notion that Jesus elevates certain parts of scripture over others is an important one. It opens us to the possibility that while the whole Bible is God's Word, some parts of God's Word are to be given greater weight. If the Bible wasn't flat for Jesus, it shouldn't be for us either.

LENSES CHANGE

It's a crisp late fall evening; I'm standing in the bleachers at a local sporting event. It's cold, so I instinctively cup my hands around my mouth and blow into them. My breath delivers hot air and warms my hands.

Later I go to the concession to get a cup of coffee. I burn my mouth on the first sip. So I open the lid and blow on the coffee. My breath delivers cold air.

The exact same breath delivers both hot and cold air.

Yet the temperature of my breath has not changed. How is this possible? The answer is context. My breath did not change, but my environment did and when it did it altered both the purpose, power, and meaning of my breath.

The story of my breath is a way of describing what happens when our lenses change. Sometimes a lens changes because we begin to question it on our own rational grounds. Other times we adopt new lenses because a teacher convinces us to change them. But sometimes they change because the context or environment changes around us.

A dramatic or traumatic life experience is enough to crack a lens and replace it with a new one. A passage of scripture that once meant one thing to us changes, deepens, or expands because we have now had a new experience. This is how lenses function. It's one of the reasons two people can view the exact same event, verse, or experience and come up with opposite or opposing conclusions.

A few years ago I was rocking my infant daughter back to sleep at 2 a.m. I had already been up for two hours and was almost falling asleep standing up. I was reminded of a documentary I'd seen on interrogation and torture techniques, in which they found that one of the most effective methods of torture was sleep deprivation: dull but incredibly debilitating.

The next day I read a Psalm that said "God does not slumber." I had read it a few times before and all it ever meant to me was that God is always watching and you can't trick God. God is the ever-vigilant watchman, and I am the criminal God is looking for. But in the quiet moment of my sleep-less fog, I realized that perhaps this passage means something different.

I was suffering for the sake of my daughter. A large part of parenting is suffering for the sake of another, fueled by love. I stayed awake so she could sleep. In light of this new experience, it sud-denly occurred to me that the passage about God not sleeping was not about God's judging eye, but rather God's willingness to do for us what I did for my daughter. A sleepless God may be an image of one who suffers so we don't have to. This experience of my sleeplessness for the sake of my daughter's rest was a new context for me. And it provided me with a new lens by which to see things I didn't see before. It was like seeing the leaves on the tree for the first time.

Our experiences affect how we perceive things. A marriage, the end of a marriage, the loss of a job, an encounter with extreme poverty or brutal injustice, the birth of a child, the sickness of a child, a confrontation with failure, or a realization of damage we have done to ourselves and others—all these and more have the power to shape the way we read and understand the messages of the Bible. Each of these experiences may color or replace our lenses, causing us to see new truths in the Bible we never saw before, while diminishing other truths that were once of great importance to us.

The Bible does not change any more than our breath. But our experiences, assumptions, and environments inevitably do. And when they do, it changes what we see in the Bible.

We all have lenses, but not all lenses are created equal. Some help us see more, some cause us to see less. This is partly what Jesus was up to when he answered the Pharisees' questions. He was offering a new prescription. Perhaps this Jesus-centered lens is one we should adopt. One that elevates love of God, and love of neighbor and self as the interpretive keys to the Bible.

I have studied the Bible through various lenses and held on to some of them for years. All of them were valuable, but some were more helpful than others. Several that I've been working with lately inform my reading of the Bible and shape the ideas in this book:

1. *The Bible is a story, but it is also a debate.* It records a debate and a conversation about who God is. There is disagreement about what God says, what God wants, and what God doesn't say or want. This debate should not be minimized; it should be welcomed for its wisdom. To this day, we continue the debate and conversation, trusting that it deepens and expands our understanding of God rather than hinders it. I have no interest in trying to harmonize the message of the Bible. The wrinkles, conflict, and contradictions are an important part of the story—or debate.

2. *The Bible records an ongoing expansion in human development.* The Bible emerged over a period of several thousand years. And as it did, people encountered new life conditions, technologies, cultures, and religions. These interactions demanded that people grow, develop, and incorporate more complex and inclusive worldviews. This means that the parts of the Bible written in more recent history will reflect different beliefs

and convictions than the parts written in a more distant history. What some call contradictions, I often read as a necessary and inevitable expansion in consciousness.

3. *I read the Bible through Jesus mostly.* Whatever disagreements about God are found in the Bible, I use Jesus as the final arbiter of the debate. He modeled the reality that some things in the Bible matter more than other things (i.e., the Greatest Commandment). I interpret nearly everything in scripture through his life and teachings. This may seem overly simple. It doesn't solve every problem; sometimes it even creates new ones. But on balance, I've found it has helped me more than any other lens.

4. *The Bible is God's Word, but not exclusively so.* Experience, tradition, creation, reason, relationship, suffering, joy, and countless other things may also contain and convey God's Word in the world. The Bible is a medium fixed in time and space, but God's Word is not bound by these things. We must be careful not to confuse God's Word and the Bible as one and the same. The Bible contains God's Word, but that Word is much bigger than the Bible.

These are just a few of the lenses I have consciously chosen. I probably use others without awareness. Certainly my life experiences have radically shaped my lenses on life. Everything that follows in this book is informed by these and other lenses.

Over the years I have found most of the debates about the Bible, doctrine, theology, and religion are not actually debates about what the Bible says. They are in fact debates informed by competing unconscious lenses. Until we understand and name these hidden assumptions, our debates are destined for perpetual gridlock. Only when we understand what we and others see *through* can we push beyond the endless polarizations. By becoming conscious of the lenses that each of us has chosen, even if we don't agree on them, we have a chance at a productive conversation about what the Bible says and what it might mean for our lives.

Understanding and owning our lenses helps us in an unexpected way. Once we see them we can actually start to get beyond them, past the merchant to the river itself, to the Living Water Jesus promised.

WIND AND THE SAILS

What Jesus Reveals about Religion

Jen had a warm but weary countenance and a smile that came from habit more than heart. She was struggling in her relationships. Her kids were acting out. At dinnertime she rarely sat down to eat because if her children complained about the food, she would make them something else just so she wouldn't have to endure their bickering and meltdowns. Sometimes she would prepare four different meals in a night. She was a delightful woman, but the cost of this way of living was beginning to show. Despite the smile, she was deeply unhappy.

She came to see me for some help. What became clear during our time together is she needed to learn to say no; she needed to learn to establish boundaries and assert her own needs. She also needed courage and fortitude to endure blowback.

Boundaries are a crucial ingredient in the development of our identity. Boundaries are what determine where I end and you begin. It's how I learn to feel safe and develop a sense of self apart from others. A clear sense of personal identity is the rudder by which we navigate through life.

Identity functions in a similar way for institutions, including religious ones. Boundaries are what help to create a sense of security and identity. They provide a way for members to know if they belong. In a religious setting, boundaries are expressed as beliefs. A religion promotes its members' beliefs in certain ideas, helping them define themselves. This is one reason why beliefs are so important to people, especially members of a religion. Without secure beliefs people lose the boundaries that provide the needed identity, stability, and protection.

For religions, boundaries and beliefs are like the banks of a river. Without the banks the river might become a stagnant pond or worse, a destructive flood. With them it is contained and directed. Clearly agreed-upon beliefs are designed to keep its members safe, together, and moving in the same direction.

The disconcerting part about the life and teachings of Jesus is that he repeatedly pushed, subverted, and overturned the established beliefs and boundaries of religion. Jesus wasn't opposed to the riverbanks; he just knew that eventually all rivers merge with the ocean. And no banks can contain the ocean. Jesus consistently stepped over the riverbanks to show us how to splash in the river. He knew the river would quench our thirst, and that it takes us somewhere incredible. Eventually the river runs and merges with the expansive and untamable ocean—the experience of life that resides beyond the limits of doctrine, boundaries, and fear.

The book of John tells us that Jesus attended a wedding. In those days weddings lasted for several days, and it was customary for the finest wine to be served first, and then when the guests had become a little tipsy, the host brought out the cheaper wine.

This particular wedding must have been some celebration, because the host ran out of wine early. So Jesus decided to intervene and tell the servants to fill nearby jars with water, then he turned that water into wine. And the party continued.

This is actually the first miracle of Jesus recorded in the book of John. It's his first impression, the inaugural address. Given this fact, it's a very strange miracle.

It is difficult to imagine that the God of all creation, the source and summit of all life, would make his first display of ultimate and unrestrained power in the flesh by helping people maintain their buzz. Without the feeding of the five thousand, people would starve. Without the healing of a blind man, he would never be able to see. Without turning water into wine? People would sober up. What a strange miracle. But there is more to it than meets the eye.

In those days, wine was served from one of two containers. Either a wineskin—a small carrier of wine made of animal skin—or something called an amphora. Amphorae were more commonly used for larger gatherings, like weddings. These were big clay jars. The mouth of the jar was much larger than a typical bottle for easy refill. But they were also narrow enough that they could be corked to preserve and transport the wine. They even had handles on the sides for easy pouring.

So here's the scene. The wedding planners have run out of wine. They have a whole lot of empty wine jars—amphorae—lying around, and in John 2:6–7 it says, "Nearby stood six stone water jars, the kind used by the Jews for ceremonial washing, each holding from twenty to thirty gallons. Jesus said to the servants, 'Fill the jars with water.'"

This is quite unexpected. Jesus chooses six stone water jars, not the wine jars, and John gives an important detail, to make sure that we don't miss the message: "*The kind used by the Jews for ceremonial washing.*" Jesus wants the wine in those stone jars, not in the far more obvious and user-friendly choice of the readily available empty amphorae.

The ceremonial stone jars were basically immovable, standing about four feet tall and equally wide, with thick walls, to be used as basins for ceremonial hand washing. They would periodically be refilled during the party, because the process of ritual cleaning had to be repeated to ensure cleanliness throughout the week of celebration.

Jesus was Jewish, and for the Jews ritual cleaning was less about literal hygiene and more about spiritual purification. You could not be in the presence of God, who is Holy, unless you were pure, ritually clean. Nearly everything about Jewish religious practice and belief at that time revolved around this issue of purification. Purity was established through separation or boundaries. Two things might each be clean, but the moment you put them together you would contract something called *Tuma*—a spiritual disease to describe the condition of ritual uncleanness. The practice of keeping kosher is largely about avoiding *Tuma*. The key is separation. You can eat meat, and you can eat milk products. But you can't eat meat and milk products together. So, no cheeseburgers. The reason is that in order to eat meat you must kill, which means meat requires death. Milk comes from something living, to sustain life. Meat is death and milk is life. Life and death are to be kept separate.

Water in stone jars is good; the jars are necessary for purification. Wine at a wedding is great, even necessary for celebration. But water and wine are not to be mixed or both are defiled and people will be unclean.

Jesus went out of his way to needlessly mix two things that should have remained separate. His miracle actually violated a fundamental boundary and challenged a belief system. By turning the water in the purity jars into wine he contaminated both according to religious boundaries. What makes this miracle so astounding isn't just the change in chemical composition from one liquid into another, but the flagrant disregard for religious boundaries.

Why would Jesus do this incredibly disrespectful, offensive, and irresponsible thing? Why wouldn't he just fill the amphorae with water and turn that into wine?

The reason takes us back to riverbanks and the ocean. Jesus was always pushing people beyond the banks and into the river. He knew these methods would get people wet and they might even get upset. But he also knew the current would take them directly into the ocean of God's heart, a vast expanse where no boundary can contain or tame the inexhaustible joy and love found there.

This inaugural miracle sets the stage for his way of operating in the world. It frames his entire ministry. Jesus repeatedly disregards the boundaries established by religion. He heals people on the Sabbath. He speaks with and even touches women, which rabbis didn't do unless they were family. He interacts with and heals people whose races his religion despised, like the Samaritans. He kept moving people toward the vast ocean, beyond the narrow confines of the riverbanks.

WHAT DOESN'T BEND, BREAKS

Religions have a tendency to get stuck. Institutions aren't made to stay limber; they seek preservation, which is a noble and important function. Thus, the trajectory of any religion is always to become brittle. A basic law is at work in most things we humans create: whatever the intended purpose of our creation, when overextended, it can reverse on itself. For example, a car is designed to speed up transportation, but too many cars create traffic jams, which slow us down. The Christian religion is intended to preserve and perpetuate the good news of Jesus. But when it becomes overextended, when the impulse is to preserve the institution rather than the message, it begins to suffocate that message.

The difficulty with the Christian religion is that our institution is centered on the person of Jesus, and Jesus consistently undermined the natural inertia of institutions. He was the embodiment of pure, unbridled creative force.

Creativity is often disruptive. It has little interest in preservation; it is about making new things and making things new. Creation by nature is always expanding, growing, and unfolding. Jesus upends, revives, and restores the malleability of our rigid religions.

I lived in California for a few years. I learned that the best way to prevent an earthquake from destroying a building is to construct the building so that it can sway and swoon, bend and wobble. Make the foundation of the building less rigid and it will ride the earthquake rather than try to resist it. The building is designed to go with the flow.

The same is true of our religion—what doesn't bend may break. This simple lesson in physics applies even to our souls. The ability to bend and flex matters. We might say blessed are the flexible for they won't get bent out of shape.

We shouldn't confuse the ability to bend with weakness, however. Bamboo possesses a dramatic flexibility, but it's known for having exceptional strength. After the atomic bomb was unleashed on Hiroshima, the bamboo in the city showed little damage amid the ruins. Sometimes strength is in the flexibility.

One of the most difficult aspects of following Jesus is that he will often upend, strip, or remake the things we have grown attached to, dependent on, and comfortable with. Even the religion that bears his name is not immune from his subversive tendencies when Christianity becomes a force for preservation rather than creation. The excessive fixation on boundaries and preservation is often the very force that prevents people from finding the river.

While Jesus did not come to preserve or fossilize, he also didn't come to throw out all conventions or boundaries. As disruptive as Jesus can be, he is not in the business of destroying the good that went before. He did not smash the stone jars. Instead he included the jars in the new thing he was creating. He used them in a different way. What Jesus did may have been offensive to those steeped in the traditions of religion, but it wasn't destructive. It was profoundly creative.

Nearly everything in our lives has a tendency to become sticky. We get attached easily, and Jesus will gently but persistently help us release our grasp on what we think we need. He shows us how little of what we feel we need is actually necessary.

This miracle is a metaphor for the way God's creative impulse operates in us, for how growth happens. We don't have to leave everything behind; some things we will keep, some things will function differently in our lives, and some things we won't need or even want anymore.

To immerse ourselves in this river of Living Water requires a kind of bamboo soul, one that has strength born of flexibility. The question is, how open and limber is our soul? How prepared are we for God to fill our sacred jars with extravagant wine? What if the things that offend us actually present a possibility for our growth? What if the loss of things we loved is a chance to reclaim the simplicity of God's love? Our hearts must remain malleable to be able to receive God's gifts.

The capacity to hold our religious assumptions, tendencies, and preconceived rules with an open hand and heart is the posture required to experience the wild, beautiful, and unpredictable ocean that Jesus came to show us.

THE WIND DOESN'T NEED A SAIL

Given the tendency for Jesus to mess with our religious boundaries, assumptions, and attachments, perhaps we would be wise to remember that Jesus and the religion that bears his name are not the same thing.

If Christ is the wind, then Christianity is a sail.

You'll find a lot of sails and boats at a sailing regatta. The shape and size of each sail varies, and some are much better than others at catching the wind. Some sailors are much better at wielding the sail.

But there is only and always one wind. It shows no loyalty or favoritism. A sailor could paint the word WIND on the boat's sail, claiming that this sail belongs to the wind. The sailor could write songs about the wind. Nothing is wrong with this. But the wind will not belong to that sail, any more than the sun would claim to depend on the earth. A sail without wind is merely a limp flag. But wind without a sail is still the wind.

The relationship is only one way.

Just because Christianity claims Jesus as its own does not mean that Jesus claims Christianity as his own. Christ does not bind himself to a religion, any more than wind binds itself to a sail.

Nor is Jesus opposed to religion, any more than the wind is opposed to sails. He can do his work with or without religion. Christians are given the privilege of participating with him in his work, but we are not entitled to this participation merely because our religion bears his name. Our participation is born of our behaviors and actions, not of the name we give ourselves or claim as our own.

The Christian religion, with all its doctrine, dogmas, rituals, and rules is a sail, not the wind—a form, not the force. As sails go, I think it has the greatest potential to harness the wind (although I admit I have only dabbled with other sails). This is the one I've used most of my life, and I prefer it.

But over my years as a Christian, I've learned that this sail is about as useful as the one who wields it. No matter how great the sail, it can be misused and made worthless or even harmful in the hands of an unskilled sailor. At times, I have been guilty of loosening the sail until it misses the wind entirely, only to stall the boat. I've also been guilty of pulling the sail in so white-knuckle tight that the boat capsizes, leaving me cold and causing damage to my boat and the boats around me.

A proper relationship between the sail and the wind is crucial.

We must never make an idol of the sail and thereby miss the wind. But it is also a mistake to say the sail doesn't matter. Without a sail, the wind is difficult to catch. So we must learn to look first for the wind, and then to wield our sail with responsiveness and wisdom. Hold on too tight, and we capsize. Let the sail out, and we halt our movement in the world.

It is not the sail, but the wind we are after.

A MAP IN THE WILDERNESS

The Gift of Belief

A cloud of blackflies swarmed my head. These little bloodsuckers were wearing me down. Legend has it that the blackflies of the North can even swarm and kill a moose! The back of my neck, the only exposed skin, was scabbing over with evidence of their effects. I should say too that trail mix five days in a row is a poor excuse for food. So I was cranky, but that's camping.

We were about halfway through a canoe trip. The map we were using was about twenty years old, and we had used it to plan a challenging route. We chose what looked like a slow-moving river that we would paddle upstream for a few days. It bypassed several long portages where we'd have to carry our gear between lakes. Then we planned to travel across two lakes, and ultimately cut our own trail to another river that would take us all the way back down to a pickup location. The downriver portion of the trip would be our reward.

As we paddled upriver, we ran into repeated beaver dams along the way. Each time we would crawl out onto the dam, lug our heavy metal canoes out of the water, and haul them over. It was always precarious, trying not to slip a leg between the broken branches and slick logs. Then we'd cautiously lumber back in the canoe without tipping it and paddle around the bend only to encounter another dam. Shouting its name was enough to express our feelings about it.

After about a week of this, we finally arrived on the shores of the last lake we needed to cross before cutting a trail. We set our gear down on the shore and peered out over the lake to discover a very strange thing.

The lake wasn't there.

The lake bed was there, but the water was not. It had become a sagging field of deep sludge and tall reeds set amid the forest. We explored the perimeter of the lakeshore, hoping we could portage our gear around the edge, but the forest was too dense and the lake bed too long. After a lot of deliberation, we turned around and headed back down the way we came.

The map is not the territory.

Maps can never contain or convey everything about a territory. Our map had all the dimensions, the coordinates, and distances exactly right, but it couldn't plot the beaver dams or blackflies and it didn't know that the lake had recently gone missing. Our map wasn't bad, just limited. Ultimately we had to go on our own experience of the terrain.

DEMANDS OF THE TERRITORY

We accumulate maps for various purposes in life. And people are always eager to give us new ones. Maps for better relationships, maps for making money, maps for how to lose weight and stay healthy. These are the "how-tos," the "proven principles," dogmas and doctrines for living.

Religions are master purveyors of maps. Their maps are very ancient, and come in the form of theology, doctrine, belief statements, and creeds. Like any map, they can help to keep us from being led astray. But even these maps can't tell us everything.

In the book of John chapter 8, some religious people catch a woman committing adultery and bring her before Jesus. The crowd tells Jesus that they are about to stone her as the law commands. They appeal to the authority of the map. They are essentially saying to Jesus, "Our trusted map says we should stone her. Are you going to doubt that?"

Jesus begins to draw in the dirt, contemplating the terrain. Then he looks up and says (loosely translated), "For a moment, set the map aside and tell me what you see. Look at your own experience for a minute. Have you ever sinned? If not, then you should follow the map without consequence. But if you have, and you follow what the map says, then a stone might be headed your way shortly." At that point the crowd is quite willing to set the map aside in lieu of the territory. A wise choice.

In another encounter, the Pharisees, the master cartographers, confront Jesus about how he shouldn't have healed people on the Sabbath. The map, it appears, forbids healing on that day. But Jesus responds simply, "The Sabbath was made for humans, not humans for the Sabbath." Sometimes the realities that confront us demand that we set the map aside. The map is there to aid you; you don't exist for the sake of the map.

Throughout his ministry, Jesus says, "You have heard it said...but I say to you..." Or we might put it this way: "You know the map says this, but I'm telling you the territory demands something more of you."

BELIEVING TO KNOWING

Another way to describe this is to observe the difference between believing and knowing. Believing is about what we think, knowing is about our experience.

A belief is an idea, a conviction, or a rule that may or may not be universally true. Beliefs are faith-based assumptions, which may be subject to change. We develop or adopt a belief either because someone we trust tells us to, or the Bible seems to say it, or reason supports it. But until we've experienced it, it remains only a possibility, a speculation. Possibilities should be held with an open hand, perhaps with some humility and even humor. Who knows—we might be wrong about what we believe.

But knowing is different. Knowing is not an idea; it is an experience. If someone pinches me, I don't believe they pinched me, I know it. I experienced it. It doesn't reside in my head, it's in my body. No debate.

If believing is the map, then knowing is the territory.

If believing is the menu, then knowing is the meal. And the point of a life with God is ultimately to enjoy the meal, not just to peruse the menu.

Things happen in life that can change what we believe. We encounter a missing lake and are forced to correct our map, or find a newer one. This can be an unnerving process, mostly because we have become very dependent on our maps.

However, it's not as strange as it seems. If you could go back in time and have a conversation with yourself when you were ten, fifteen, or twenty years younger, would you be talking to someone who shares your exact same beliefs or worldview? Or have you shifted, grown, deepened, and expanded? Have you always believed everything you believe right now in exactly the same way? Or has it changed?

Over time, and through our life experiences, we often learn to amend our understanding of life. The more we experience in life, the more we are able to alter the maps to more accurately reflect what we come to know. One of the great gifts of knowing, or experiencing something directly, is that we no longer have to think about or debate it. It just is. This brings a measure of peace, clarity, and even humble certainty.

It is better to know than to believe. It is better to move from merely thinking about God in the right ways to experiencing God deeply and directly. The Living Water that Jesus promised must be *known*, experienced.

Nothing is wrong with believing. But to assume that belief is all we need is about as useful as looking at a menu and claiming it's as good as eating the meal. Religion directs our attention to the menu, but we will find Christ in the kitchen.

Knowing is powerful. Sometimes it can cause us to rethink our beliefs about God. But it can work in the opposite direction too. Sometimes we may have a belief about God, but have yet to experience it. When we do finally experience it, the belief essentially disappears. In a sense it is no longer necessary. The intellectual speculation is replaced with a deep and humble knowing.

TRUST DESPITE THE EVIDENCE

I first learned to sail in middle school at a weeklong camp. The first day of the camp we never even went outside. In the middle of summer, we sat in a classroom with bay windows that looked out over a gorgeous lake on a sunny day—a special kind of torture for teenagers.

The instructors spent the day teaching us proper sailing terminology and various techniques and rules of sailing. They taught us that the big pole in the middle was called the "mast." The bar jutting out horizontally was called the "boom." The boat had a "starboard" and a "port" side, not a right and a left side. They taught us that when the sail flaps in the wind that's called "luffing," and if you see that happening you aren't properly harnessing the wind. You do that by pulling in the "sheet," the rope that controls the angle of the boom.

Everything they told me, I believed. I trusted the instructors because they had firsthand experience with sailing. When we finally got out there in the boats, I noticed at one point that my sail was luffing, so I pulled the sheet in hard, just like they told me. The sail stopped luffing, just like they said, the boat started moving and picking up speed, just like they said, and then shortly after the boat keeled over and dumped us in the drink, *not* like they said. We righted the boat, climbed back in and went after the wind again. We did what they said and found ourselves in the water a few more times.

Now, it would have been easy to conclude that the instructors were liars. What I believed was directly contradicted by my experience. It would have been easy to conclude that what I now knew was not what I was taught to believe.

But I persisted in trusting that they knew something I didn't. I assumed I must be doing something wrong. So I kept trying. Eventually, I noticed that I needed to release the sail gently as a way to stabilize the boat when it started to keel up. I needed to become respectful and responsive to the wind, rather than rigid and locked. And when I did, the boat was kind to us, and we stayed dry. Just like they said. It was amazing.

I didn't believe anymore; I knew. I went from believing to knowing. From trusting to tasting. From reading the menu to eating the meal. And even though my experience at first seemed to contradict what I believed, I persisted in my belief until I came to know.

BECOME A KNOWER

I became a Christian in the fifth grade. I professed my faith in Jesus and believed the things I read and was taught. I believed that God loved me because my pastors told me. I couldn't point to a firsthand experience, but the idea was deeply appealing.

There were times in life that I didn't feel like there was much evidence for this belief. It wasn't always easy to believe. When I was a sophomore in college at home for Easter break, my dad and I were talking in the backyard. I was stressed and full of anxiety about my future. I didn't know what I wanted to do in life and felt like time was running out. It's not something I talked about much, but I thought about it frequently.

My dad is a man steeped in God. For decades he has been waking up at 5 a.m. to spend hours in periods of silence, journaling, contemplative reading, and prayer. He is highly attentive to the Spirit. But he rarely talks about it unless he is asked. He didn't often initiate spiritual conversations.

On that day, as the sun streamed through the tall trees, he turned to me and said, "Shane, I have this sense that there is some kind of a knot in your soul. And I'd like to pray for it. And I have this sense that it is in your chest, so I'd like to place my hands on your chest and pray silently." He stood at my side, facing me. He placed one hand over my heart and the other on my back and stood for a few moments. The warmth of his hands radiated in me. I vividly remember this feeling that something in me uncoiled. I fought back tears, but they streamed anyway. After a few moments I could feel the knot release.

In that moment I didn't just believe that God loved me. I had direct experience of a Presence, a Love, a Peace that was bigger than I had ever known. I already knew my dad loved me, but this was different. I could feel a connection to something much larger than my own father. I cannot prove it for anyone else, but it was profoundly real to me.

Each of us will take the path from believing to knowing on our own. This experience of knowing was meant for only me. When I was there, all thoughts and debates about the nature of God or God's existence simply fell away. And I merely rested in my newfound knowledge.

There is a humble and easy certainty in knowing. No need to debate.

When Jesus commands his followers to go and make disciples, this is not a command to make believers; it is a call to make followers, students, or learners. A student is progressing, just like I was in sailing school, from believing to knowing. Jesus wants people to know, not just to believe. He wants people to experience God's love, rather than just think rightly about it.

What we believe and what we know are in a dynamic relationship. They shape us and what we assume to be possible. Like my canoe trip, sometimes our experience of the terrain teaches us that our maps are off base, limited, or applied the wrong way. In these times, we must set beliefs aside and let our experience deepen and expand our beliefs.

Like my sailing experience, sometimes we must hold on to our beliefs despite evidence to the contrary. When the end of a relationship, a job, or the loss of our health confronts us, it is easy to doubt that God is present or even cares about us. It is natural to lose heart when our boat capsizes and life leaves us cold, wet, and even wounded. In those times, we must trust. Trust that God's love is not fiction, but the truest reality. We must hold intrepidly to this belief, until the day we come to *know* its truth. The day we taste the sweet inner consolation and peace of God in the face of difficult life circumstances.

Then we become more than a believer; we become a *knower* of God.

SHEDDING THE SWADDLE

The Limits of Belief

In the ninth chapter of John's gospel, Jesus is walking along and sees a man who has been blind from birth. Jesus approaches him, spits on the ground, makes mud with his saliva, and spreads this mud on the man's eyes. Then he tells the man to go and wash his face in a nearby pool. The blind man does as he is told, and suddenly he can see.

This event causes serious commotion and people in town bring the man to the Pharisees. John 9:14 tells us why it was such a problem: "Now it was a Sabbath day when Jesus made the mud and opened his eyes" (ESV).

Then a long and involved courtroom drama unfolds about the law. The reason? It's a sin to do pretty much anything on the Sabbath, including healing or making mud. Jesus did a lot of healing. But this healing is very unique. Not only because he performed the healing on the Sabbath, but for another reason.

The blind man didn't ask to be healed.

It was done entirely on the initiative of Jesus

and involved a particular kind of motivation. Jesus healed him in a way that involved work. He didn't have to make mud cakes to heal this guy. Jesus healed a woman by doing nothing other than brushing past her in a crowd. He healed a little girl miles away just by speaking. So Jesus could have simply winked and restored the man's sight, thereby remaining utterly Sabbath compliant. Or if he wanted to involve the labor-intensive theatrics of mud pies, he could have just waited a few hours until the Sabbath was over. It's not like this was an urgent need. The man had been blind since birth, wasn't asking to be healed, and wasn't getting any more blind. Jesus is up to something here, and it's only partly about healing. Jesus was putting a stick in the wheel of the religious establishment by violating the boundaries they had established.

When my daughter was an infant, I learned early on that she slept a lot better when she was swaddled. If you're not familiar with the technology of a swaddle, it is basically a baby straightjacket made with a blanket. The technique, when done properly, completely immobilizes the child's limbs, while still allowing for breathing and blood flow. There should be no wiggle room at all. It looks terribly uncomfortable, but infants love it. For her it was the only way to sleep through the night. It imitated what she was used to; she had spent her entire life in very tight quarters.

A few months later, we noticed that she was no longer sleeping very well. One night I loosened up the swaddle a bit to see what would happen. She pushed and kicked her limbs free and then fell fast asleep. She had outgrown swaddling. What was once helpful for sleep became a hindrance. In the beginning it gave her a sense of security, but eventually it was restrictive.

In the life of faith, beliefs function a bit like a blanket. Early on they are given to us as a swaddle, often wrapped tightly around us with warnings not to play fast and loose. They are designed to keep us safe, but as we grow, beliefs must unfold—be examined and understood more deeply and differently. If they do not, either the belief is torn or the soul stops growing.

ROOM TO GROW

Throughout the Gospels, Jesus has a habit of helping religious people loosen their swaddles. Deliberately breaching boundaries and protocol seems to be one of his favorite ways of doing this.

In healing the blind man, Jesus was stripping the swaddle off the Sabbath and confronting the swaddlers, the religious leaders.

The Sabbath was at the heart of Jewish religious practice. And Jesus took direct aim at the way it had come to function in his society and religion. His treatment of the Sabbath served as a metaphor for the more general critique Jesus was leveling. The religion of his day with its practices, rituals, and regulations had become restrictive to the point of stunting growth.

It obstructed the view of the river.

Jesus is not necessarily against the practices of the religion; he is against the way they function. This is why he says in Mark 2:27, "The Sabbath was made for people, not people for the Sabbath" (TNIV). The problem is not the Sabbath, but rather how you use it. So too the swaddle was made for the baby, not the baby for the swaddle.

This is an important distinction. When my daughter left the swaddle phase, we did not burn the blanket. The blanket merely changed its function. She was allowed to use or not use it as she saw fit. And for the most part she continued to use it, occasionally kicking it off when she was too warm.

The relationship my daughter had to her blanket is also found in the dynamic of beliefs in people's lives. Our beliefs are like that blanket: at times they serve us best when tightly wrapped around us. And at other times, they must be loosened to make room for growth. The trick is knowing when to do each.

THE WAY BOUNDARIES WORK

Dave was a big guy. His physical stature gave him a kind of menacing presence. He had a naturally abrasive personality, strong opinions, and was demonstrative in his anger. Most people, including his close friends, found him intimidating, so much so that they never told him that.

One day he met Jen (the weary, overly accommodating mother who we met at the beginning of the "Wind and the Sails" chapter). She had a sweet, mouselike personality, and she found his incredible strength and protectiveness very attractive. They started dating, fell in love, and eventually married. Throughout the marriage she was very supportive, but over time she became increasingly unhappy. While this feeling grew, she never made so much as a peep about it.

After a number of years, she asked to go to

counseling. He was surprised but reluctantly agreed. By the third session, much to everyone's surprise, Jen asked for a divorce. Dave was shocked, appalled, and furious at this request. He blew up, hurled accusations, and leveled criticisms. She sat quietly, hardly wincing at his anger. Dave couldn't understand what had happened.

During the months and additional counseling that followed, he learned that throughout most of their marriage Jen had been terrified and traumatized by his anger. She had been worn down to a shell, felt nothing for him, and wanted to end the marriage.

Dave grew up with very loving parents. The way they expressed their love was by doting on him, celebrating him. He had absolutely no memory of ever being disciplined. They didn't want him to think he was unloved. One of the things he learned from them was that he could do no wrong. Throughout most of his life, his relational habits went largely unchecked. There were no limits placed around him and no one really gave him much honest feedback. Any negative criticism he received from others he easily disregarded as "their problem." For most of his life, he never saw how much he frightened people around him. And he lost the person he loved most as a result. He wasn't malicious or cruel, just unaware. And it cost him more than he wanted to pay.

Jen was raised in a very different way. She was taught how to be a servant and a good little girl. She was to remain quiet and supportive, just like her mom. Jen's parents also made it clear that Jesus values humility and demands service to others even when we don't like it. She was taught to "take up her cross" and "carry it daily." Which she did dutifully in life and marriage.

Until one day something in her simply collapsed and she couldn't carry anything anymore, including herself. She lost heart in her marriage and ended it out of survival, much to everyone's surprise— her own included. Over time, she learned the part she had played in the decline of the marriage. As a child, she never had anyone demonstrate or give her permission to have and express her own needs. She wasn't allowed to be sad or assertive. And she certainly wasn't allowed to be angry. The Bible forbids it, she was told (which is a lie).

This relationship and these two people are the products of the way boundaries functioned in their lives. Dave was never given restrictions, limits, or rules of behavior. There was nothing to push up against him and help him discover how he affected others. He never learned basic impulse control. He wasn't given the gift of restraint or swaddling early on. His anger was always unrestrained and felt internally justified. As a result, he only learned impulse control and anger management much later in life through a very hard lesson.

Jen was given a firm swaddle early on, but it was never released. She was swaddled long past the time she should have been, and was never given a chance to push her arms out and experience freedom and choice. And she suffered for many years because of it.

While they weren't able to save their marriage, they each started on a path to growth. Dave learned to practice better boundaries and impulse control, while Jen learned to move past the ones that kept her repressed and closed down.

This story is about intimate relationships but I've seen the central dynamic at work in nearly every area of life. It could be our ego, how we relate to food, drinking, sex, drugs, work, or beliefs. Every one of these issues has a developmental component. Early in life it is necessary to learn restraint, yet once impulses are checked we must shed the swaddle in order to grow.

WHEN TO BREAK FREE

If these boundaries are not applied early on, people ruin lives, their own and those of others. If boundaries never allow us to breathe, we suffocate and our evolution in God is stunted.

The lesson Jesus offers is simple. We should not despise old obediences or constraints; they help. But if left in place for too long or in the wrong way, these obediences can become pointless abuses.

We must learn to gradually release constraints that have outlived their usefulness—we must shed the swaddle if we are to grow. Knowing how and when to shed the swaddle is a matter of wisdom and experience.

Certain beliefs, practices, and boundaries serve a purpose for people at different times and in life. If we are genuinely evolving in God, we will discover that some of the things that once served us so well are no longer serving us. They may even be debilitating to our relationship with God. We are invited to courageously shed them so we may become more of our true selves in God.

This may sound odd, even scary. How do we know when we are ready to break out of the swaddle or whether we are rejecting a necessary discipline? How do we know if we are going too easy, or too hard on ourselves?

Consider my daughter in her swaddle. When I loosened the swaddle, she broke free with force. But she did not rid herself of the blanket entirely. She held on to it for warmth. And she was able to relax and fall fast asleep. When we took her out of the swaddle too soon, she would often continue to squirm and squawk. She was neither relaxed nor content.

You'll know you've shed your own old beliefs at the right time when you are still able to appreciate them. You may experience an initial burst of energy or even feel anger when you first break free. This is normal. However, this won't last forever. In time it will be replaced by a sense of appreciation for how protective those outgrown beliefs were. You'll begin to see their function more clearly and how well they served you for a time. You'll even be able to recognize how useful such convictions still are for others.

An indication you have shed restraint too soon is when you lose all discipline. Or if you feel compelled to force everyone to shed their swaddles as you have done. These are forms of squirming and squawking, and they are indications that you are rebelling rather than growing.

Perhaps it is easier in life to say *better safe than sorry* or *when in doubt, err on the safe side*. However, remember that Jesus is always up to something in our lives. We are being beckoned to evolve in God. Some security blankets in our lives need to be relinquished.

Do you know your swaddle? And are you ready to let Jesus untie it? Can you kick it away and let it go? You get to choose between safety and growth. Growth is rarely safe.

TOUCHING THE STOVE

The Way of Fear and Love

Those of us raised in Christianity often live with a lot of fear. Fear that we are doing it wrong (whatever "it" is). Fear that some unfamiliar idea might hurt us. Fear that God may not like who we are, or what we've done, or what we think. Fear that a particular interpretation of the Bible is hurting the Bible or even God. Fear that we, or others, might be offending God, who apparently has quite fragile feelings, and a hair-trigger temper. Some religious people are even afraid that other people are not frightened enough.

Fear is not unique to the religious, but I have found it to be particularly acute among us. When people come to me with questions or looking for help, fear lurks behind many problems and inquiries—overt and subtle. Fear is driving us in conscious and unconscious ways.

The fact that we Christians carry around so much fear is bizarre to me. Our religion clearly invites us to live without fear. In 1 John 4:18, the writer makes this simple observation: "There is no fear in love. But perfect love drives out fear."

When John refers to "perfect love," he uses it as a synonym for God. Elsewhere he observes that "God is love" (1 John 4:8). For John, this is not a metaphor or an analogy; he doesn't say God is *like* love, or God *has* love. He says God *is* love. When I refer to "Love" with a capital "L" in this book, I am referring, as John does, to God.

In this passage about fear and love, John is expressing an incredibly important insight about the nature of fear—that it has no place in the life of faith. So where did we get this tendency for Christianity to produce so much fear?

Fear is an important part of the Old Testament. It is understood as an essential ingredient in the development of wisdom.

> Psalm 111:10: The fear of the LORD is the beginning of wisdom.

> Prov. 1:7: The fear of the LORD is the beginning of knowledge.

> Job 28:28: The fear of the Lord—that is wisdom.

According to these passages, fear is essential for wisdom. Yet according to John it has no place in love. How can this be? If I want wisdom I must learn fear; if I want Love I must rid myself of fear.

But if I want both, what should I do with this contradiction?

Some may say this is not a contradiction because the *object* of this Old Testament fear is specifically the *Lord*. The only problem is that John doesn't make an exception here. He doesn't say "There is no fear in love, except for fear of the Lord—that kind of fear is okay." He simply says that fear of any kind simply cannot be found in Love. Love by its nature rids us of all fear. The nature of Love is that it cannot contain fear.

Others may suggest that when the Bible tells us to "fear the Lord" it is actually a reference to "respect" or "reverence." This is an invitation to feel strong awe for God, rather than be frightened. And to a degree that is true, this kind of fear is about respect. However, the central meaning and semantic range of the Hebrew word "*yirah*" is still *fear*, even *terror*. So while there is a connotation of respect, it is respect born of fear. Make no mistake about it; the original writers are talking about trembling and terror before God and God's power.

It would appear that John is saying one thing and these other passages say another. In one case fear is of no use at all, but in the other case fear is essential. So should we be afraid or shouldn't we?

One says yes, and the other says absolutely not, under any circumstances.

This conundrum is played out beautifully in a passage from Exodus, chapter 20. Verse 20 says "Moses said to the people, 'Do not be afraid. God has come to test you, so that the fear of God will be with you to keep you from sinning.'"

Okay, got it. So I shouldn't be afraid, so that I can be afraid. And that fear that I'm not supposed to have will keep me from sinning. Clear as mud. A recent experience showed me another way to look this.

FEARS ARE LEARNED

When my daughter was two she liked to be held a lot. She was particularly keen on being held at the most inconvenient times. Chief among them is when I needed to cook. I would hold her for a while, but at a certain point my arm would get tired and I would set her on the counter next to the stove so she could watch me cook. This seemed to work for her, but it always made me a little nervous. Early on I started to instill in her an awareness of how dangerous the stove was. "Do not touch the stove. It's very hot. It will hurt you." I repeated this several times in a stern manner. Soon she learned the stove was dangerous. She was not naturally afraid of the burner; I had to help her learn how to be afraid. For my daughter, fear of the stove was the beginning of wisdom.

The same fears were imparted to me when I was a toddler to protect me. As I grew, I learned that the stove wasn't always hot or dangerous. I then needed to revise my universal fear of stoves. When I was older I learned to read the contextual clues. I would inspect the color of the burner, or place my hand just above it to see if I could detect heat. I might even touch it quickly to see if it was hot. All these things could tell me if it was okay to touch the stove.

At each developmental stage, certain rules apply, and at later stages the rules must be understood in new ways in order to grow. To stay safe, early in life we learn fear, but as we mature we must leave the fear behind or we become paralyzed or pathological. If a twenty-year-old is frightened of stoves in the same way he was as a two-year-old, we have a problem.

Consider once again the two passages that seem to contradict each other. One that says we shouldn't fear, the other that says fear is the beginning of wisdom. Is it possible that both these passages are actually true? Each is true at different times and in different situations. What if this is actually about faith development?

Fear is a developmental ingredient in the life of faith. It is useful in learning to prevent harm and nurture wisdom. Like a bodyguard, it protects us from wandering too far afield and helps us develop basic impulse control. Those of us who never learn to control our impulses may fail to manage our emotional lives, struggle with addiction, or do damage to others. Fear helps prevent these and other dangers in life.

But fear also has some serious limits.

THE MOVE TOWARD LOVE

In the Old Testament passages, you'll notice an important progression in the way fear operates. They say "Fear of the Lord is the *beginning* of wisdom." Fear seems to serve as a catalyst or starting point. Wisdom may *begin* with fear, but it does not end there.

The first stage of faith development often begins in fear, but it is headed somewhere else— toward Love.

Those who do learn some basic impulse control and have stabilized, healthy patterns of behavior, are prepared for the next stage of growth. And this is where it gets tricky. In the next stage, the rules actually change.

As we mature, we learn that fear moves from being something that protects us to something that imprisons us.

It moves from being an ally to an adversary.

It moves from something that helps to something that hurts.

Fear plays an important role in our development, but it also may choke our growth if we get stuck there.

This first stage of development is a much safer place to be; it is about protection. But as we grow, we are more and more moved and opened by Love, or God. In simple terms, we could say that fear is about closure and contraction, whereas Love is about opening and expansion. Love by nature is free from fear.

This process of becoming opened by Love can be unnerving, and it is not for the faint of heart. Doubts emerge when what we thought were solid foundations begin to feel like shifting sands beneath our feet. Love opens us more and more to a freedom that moves us beyond self-justification, self-protection, and self-preservation. Any time boundaries are dropped or even changed, it can feel threatening, but it is essential if we are to grow.

WHAT LOVE REQUIRES

Jazz is an improvisational art form. It has the potential to be unpredictable, and the music bends and morphs and flows in completely spontaneous harmony, intentional dissonance, and liberating beauty.

But this kind of liberated beauty does not come without decades of practice. An aspiring jazz musician must first master the scales, understand the laws governing music theory, and work to develop proper form. If they do not, then they are limited in their ability to truly unleash the catalytic capacity of the musical form. Even if they're a prodigy, their full potential is rooted first in mastery of some basic rules.

Once you learn the rules, if you never learn to break them, you are unlikely to create fresh, spontaneous beauty or truth with your art. You remain a proficient executor of musical notes, effectively arranged together in linear sequence. To be a jazz artist requires knowing and playing by the rules followed by a near total freedom from them. And it has to happen in that order or otherwise it doesn't seem to work.

This is what happens in the life of faith as well. Initially, fear may motivate us to follow rules for fear of God. But in the end we must release our fears and be moved by Love.

If we are to access the Living Water Jesus promised, ultimately Love must become the only thing that governs behavior, not fear. Once basic impulse controls are in place, we are to be moved by the spontaneous force of Love, which will sometimes abandon the very fears and even boundaries that once served us so well. Love does not do away with all boundaries; instead, it makes use of them in ways that serve the purpose of Love.

As we grow, the question we learn to ask moves from *What is right or wrong?* to *What does Love require?*

In the next stage of growth, we open more to the force of Love living our life through us. And soon we realize something very unsettling, which contradicts much of what we learned in the first stage of growth. *Love has no room for our fear.* The very things that brought us to this point are no longer welcome. Things like the fear of sin, fear of death, fear of suffering, fear of moral relativism, fear of heresy, fear of scarcity in the world, fear of not having enough money, love, sex, life, or time.

Most of these fears are learned or taught. Infants don't come out of the womb afraid of everything; that gets imparted later. Our path to God ultimately means shedding all fears and opening to Love.

You might ask, "Are you telling me that sometimes I need to touch the burner? Letting go of fears sounds a little dangerous!"

Yes, but be wise about when. This Love will always feel a little dangerous. It will be particularly threatening to one part of us—the ego. That thing which seeks self-preservation. The movement of this Love is unpredictable, like the wind. It requires that we develop the skills to become responsive to its movement. We must learn the act of ongoing discernment because there may come a time when it calls us to do what appears to be self-destructive, like leaving a well-paying job to pursue another purpose, or changing our lifestyle to raise children.

Or it may require something even more dramatic.

Look what happened when Jesus followed the call of Love. Love demanded that he break the rigid rules of religion and he suffered for it. He ended up on a cross. And yet even there his heart was fearless, wide open to boundless Love, offering mercy to the very people who were killing him. Jesus shed his fear in the garden, and then he was governed by Love alone. Such Love has no knowledge of fear.

In these moments of dramatic calling in life, it may seem like this Love is destroying us. However, that is only an illusion. We experience it in this way because we have become so used to the bars of the prison that once kept us safe. But when we live according to Love we quickly learn that it is the prison that is being destroyed, not us. In reality, we are being liberated by Love.

This Love is a powerful force, even more powerful than we often imagine it.

THE OPPOSITE OF LOVE

Seated at the kitchen table, my daughter and I were working on her kindergarten homework. At the time she was learning about opposites. Her worksheet was a matching exercise that listed two word columns. Her task was to draw a line connecting the words that represented opposites. "Day" would be matched to "Night," "Happy" to "Sad," "Light" to "Darkness," and so on.

The last pairing caught my attention. We often think of darkness as the opposite of light. "Opposites" suggests that they are equal and opposing forces; however, darkness is actually the absence of light, not the opposite. You cannot remove light from a room by adding darkness. Nor can you remove darkness from a room by capturing it somehow and taking it out. The only thing that eliminates darkness is the presence of light. Darkness and light do not exist together. They have never met.

Darkness is always at the mercy of light. If you want to be rid of darkness, light a lamp.

In 1 John 4:18, he writes "There is no fear in love. But perfect love drives out fear." What John writes here is deeply insightful for two reasons. First, he does not use the expected dualism between love and hate; instead he sets *fear* at odds with Love. This is truly revealing, as it shows us that behind all hate is really a deeper problem of fear.

Second, we are shown that the relationship between love and fear is the same as that of light and darkness. Love and fear cannot occupy the same space. Moreover, Love and fear are not equal and opposing forces. Fear is always at the mercy of Love. One way to see it is that fear is actually the *absence* of Love, not the opposite. The lesson here is an important one. Love has no opposite. No force in the universe rivals it.

With such power, we might be wise to understand that ridding ourselves of fear is as simple as letting Love in. Just as darkness automatically vanishes in the presence of light, so too fear disappears in the radiance of Love.

Our life of faith may begin with fear, we may learn from it initially. But vibrant, growing faith will be marked by an ever-expanding Love, and the corresponding dissolution of fear.

OUTSIDE THE BOAT

Just Beyond Fear

3:37 a.m. is a dreadful time to see on a clock when you wake up. My three-year-old daughter is crying. I stumble into her dark room, tripping over toys, and arrive at her bedside. "What's wrong?" I ask, as sweetly as I know how, and am informed that a giant is in her room.

The nightmare is still completely real to her. She is trembling with fear.

"Giants aren't real," I explain. As I hear my words, I realize the futility of trying to explain the nonexistence of fictional characters to a three-year-old at any time, let alone this hour. "It was just a dream."

More crying. Trying to explain the fine distinctions between human states of consciousness is also not much help.

After several failed attempts at consoling her with my sage wisdom and intellectually prescient observations about the nature of reality I pick her up and hold her in my arms. "Everything is okay now. The giant is gone. I'm here. I'll protect you."

Eventually she is ready to go back to sleep but not before pointing to darkened shapes in her room, alleging the giant was back. Her fear caused her to see things that weren't there.

Fear is a powerful lens on life. When looking through fear, sometimes it causes us to see things that aren't there or it may simply distort things that are. Fear can often prevent us from seeing reality. Fear is one of the biggest barriers to getting the water from the river.

Matthew, chapter 14, tells us that the disciples of Jesus got into a boat and headed out into a lake. Meanwhile Jesus set off up a mountainside to pray by himself. Later that night, Jesus walked out onto the lake to greet them. The scene follows: "When the disciples saw him walking on the lake, they were terrified. 'It's a ghost,' they said, and cried out in fear. But Jesus immediately said to them: 'Take courage! It is I. Don't be afraid'" (Matthew 14:26–27).

In most Bibles this story is in a section all its own, usually entitled "Jesus Walks on Water." It is a spectacular miracle and yet that is perhaps the least significant thing about it. This is especially true when you think about the impact of the miracle.

What purpose did it serve? Mostly it just frightened the tar out of the disciples. The story says it's a windy night with some waves, but does not indicate the disciples were in immediate danger. If he wanted to meet up with them, why not just take another boat? Perhaps he performed this miracle as a demonstration of power. A bit gratuitous but I guess you could say it serves a purpose.

Similar to the water-into-wine miracle, the spectacle may distract us from a more profound purpose. The passage certainly points to the remarkable powers of Jesus, but it does more than that. It teaches us something about ourselves, and what is required for our freedom.

We learn in the story that the disciples are terrified because they thought they had seen a ghost. This would be a terrifying experience no doubt, but it was no ghost, it was Jesus. This is simply a case of mistaken identity. Like when your friend walks in the room and you're not expecting it and it startles you. You're not sure who this intruder is, so the body goes into a fight-or-flight response.

A CASE OF MISTAKEN IDENTITY

In June 2005, a U.S. Navy SEAL named Marcus Luttrell served in a four-man team on a mission in Afghanistan. The mission was to capture a notorious al-Qaeda leader. Through an unfortunate series of events it all went horribly wrong and a rescue team of SEALs was sent in after them. The transport rescue helicopter carrying a large team of Special Forces was shot down and within twenty-four hours Marcus Luttrell was the only SEAL still alive. It was the largest loss of SEAL life in U.S. history. His story is detailed in the book *Lone Survivor*.

In the midst of the crisis, Marcus found himself completely alone and badly injured in the barren mountains of a remote region in Afghanistan. He was relentlessly pursued by the Taliban. Against all odds, Marcus defended himself through the night from these forces. Eventually his injuries and dehydration got the best of him and, still pursued by his enemy, he was ready to make his final stand and die.

By now he could no longer stand and could barely crawl. He hardly had the strength to hold his weapon. Eventually he was lucky enough to find a small stream and began drinking from it.

Just as he was doing this, he turned to see three men standing around him, two of them with AK-47s. One was yelling at him. On instinct he raised his rifle and aimed at the one yelling who quickly dodged behind a tree. He writes:

> I was like a badly wounded animal, ready to fight to the end.... The only sensation I could react to was threat.... Cornered. Scared. Suddenly afraid of dying. Ready to lash out at anything. That was me. The only thought I had was *I'll kill these guys...just give me my chance....* I no longer knew what...was happening except that I was in some kind of fight, which I was very obviously about to lose.... I was struggling to understand what the screaming tribesman was trying to communicate. *"American! Okay! Okay!"*
>
> Finally I got it. These guys meant me no harm. They'd just stumbled on to me. It was a situation I was...unused to this past couple of days.

These men were Pashtuns, members of one of the world's oldest living tribal groups. One that observes a very strict code of honor and culture, which has helped them survive for two thousand years. They defeated the British, the former Soviet Union, India's Mogul rulers, and Alexander the Great. Today, a number of their warriors serve as the backbone of the Taliban forces. However, many Pashtuns are unsympathetic to the Taliban, these men among them. They took Marcus in as part of a strict tribal code of hospitality. They nursed him back to health, fed him, and helped him escape, all the while defending him against the Taliban.

Initially, Marcus thought they were the enemy. Their appearance shared much in common with his enemy. There was little to distinguish them from the Taliban. But they turned out to be his most loyal friends. They came not with a fist but with an open hand and saved his life. This moment of terror and lashing out seemed justified, but if he had pulled the trigger in fear, he would have certainly been killed. The people he thought were his greatest threat were actually his greatest hope. It is another case of mistaken identity. Just as the disciples thought they saw a ghost when it was actually their savior.

Sometimes what we fear the most is actually here to help us, even free us. Fear is an incredibly powerful lens. It distorts nearly everything we see. Apply the lens of fear to anything we look at—our lives, the Bible, relationships—and it can twist what we see in extraordinary ways. It can be so distorting that it can even cause us to see the opposite of what we're actually looking at.

In this way, whenever we look through fear, whatever we see may be an illusion, the magician's sleight-of-hand distracting us from reality. But if we can learn to see past this kind of fear it may actually point to our release. When we finally recognize reality, it ultimately guides us to our freedom.

When what we fear comes, we must be careful not to accept it as truth automatically. Fear is certainly telling us something, but if we act too quickly, we may miss the message. In the midst of our fear we will often hear the words of Jesus echo: "Take courage, it's me. Don't be afraid!"

If we move through fear, amazing things are possible. The moment Peter sees through the mistaken identity and recognizes it is not a ghost but his Master, his fear dissolves and he is transformed. Then Peter is able to do the impossible. Once the fear is gone, he steps out of the boat and begins to walk on the water with Jesus.

If Marcus Lutrell had acted on his fear in a raw animal instinct, he would have eliminated the possibility of his survival. Instead, he paused, just long enough for reality to reach through his distorting fear. He was patient and discovered the key to his salvation right in front of him.

When we can move through this kind of fear in life, new worlds open up to us in ways we never imagined possible.

THE OTHER SIDE OF FEAR

Standing against the wall, with furrowed brow, I studied the script in hand. "Next!" the instructor called out. In sixth grade, Space Camp wasn't about the science for me as much as the experience. They had a zero-gravity chair, a moon-walking simulator, a water rescue drill, and a full-scale simulated Space Shuttle mission. This included mission control and a Shuttle simulator, whose cockpit looked, to these young eyes, like the *Millennium Falcon* from *Star Wars*.

The simulation was run like a theater production; they gave us all a script containing two dozen roles. The campers had to try out for the parts by reading for the instructors. Based on the readings, we were cast accordingly. The most hotly coveted was that of the Shuttle Commander. Not only was this the lead role with the greatest number of lines, but that person got to occupy the captain's chair in the Shuttle. Each camper was to read for the role they most wanted.

That role was indeed very tempting. But for a dyslexic kid, the thought of a public reading struck cold dread and primordial panic in me. I don't care how cool that cockpit was.

My plan was simple: Find and request the smallest, most irrelevant role. Eventually I found the role I was born to play—Payload Specialist 3. It contained a grand total of three lines, maybe ten words. The Payload Specialist lines were easily memorized so as to feign reading for the audition. The plan went off without a hitch. A total lack of ambition coupled with the appearance of a competent reading made me a shoo-in for the one role no one wanted.

The next day an unthinkable nightmare unfolded.

The auditioning instructor came to me and said, "Shane, congratulations! You have been chosen to play the role of Shuttle Commander."

My face turned pale gray. This must be a practical joke, I insisted.

It was not. She was serious. After more pleading and invoking the inalienable right as a dyslexic to never perform public readings, she denied my requests. In a calm voice, she said, "Shane, the reason we chose you is because you were the best reader of the group. You were so poised and confident. You seemed so natural and at ease."

This would most certainly end badly. I had

masterfully embarrassed myself in far lesser public readings in the past. Grade school was full of these opportunities. The fear swallowed me whole and I resigned myself to the role. As the simulation unfolded, I read the best I could. The problem with dyslexia is you never know quite when you've read a word wrong. There was no way for me to know if I was making a fool of myself. Laughter and giggling from my peers was usually the telltale sign of error. None came. I pressed on, occasionally tripping up on a word and feeling my heart rate spike and that familiar tingle in my face that signaled that it was red.

The simulation ended. To my great surprise, I received an unusual amount of praise and positive feedback. Apparently, I did not embarrass myself. One might even say it was a success. That day, a small seed of quiet confidence was planted in me, overriding the crippling fear.

Quieting the mind and heart long enough to look beyond the fear is never easy. And this fear often returns in my life. Now it serves to beckon me deeper into one part of my calling in life as a communicator. The doorway of this fear became a vocational path in life. This fear has become a friend. This fear is now merely a quiet reminder that, while I should take my responsibility seriously, I shouldn't take myself so seriously.

BUD BEFORE BLOSSOM

The dynamic of fear in the life of faith is an important one. It must be dealt with carefully and also with some levity. When I lived in Phoenix, a large area of my front yard was comprised of a rock bed instead of grass. Maintaining a lawn in the desert is a water-intensive undertaking, so lawns usually rival the square footage of a postage stamp. It's not a great look, and has zero functionality for kids, but it's the responsible thing to do in a region whose water supply is scarce and almost entirely borrowed.

Remarkably, weeds have no trouble sprouting up. Within a few months of first moving in, I noticed weeds had started taking over my rock bed. As a dutiful suburbanite, I began pulling them so as to keep up appearances. Shortly after I got going, a neighbor on a walk passed by and gently inquired, "Oh, you're getting rid of the wildflowers?" Confused, I said, "No, just weeding the rock bed." She responded, "Those aren't weeds you're pulling. The previous owner sowed wildflower seeds all over your rock bed. And this time of year for the next few months your front yard will become a field of really beautiful yellow and orange flowers." I'm not a fan of yard work to begin with so this seemed as good an excuse as any to stop weeding. Sure enough, within a few weeks, we had a spectacular bed of brightly colored wildflowers instead of rocks. It was a great little feature of the home. I grew to anticipate and appreciate those flowers each year.

This was another case of misidentification. I mistook the flowers for weeds and set about getting rid of them. Without the neighbor's caution to let the "weeds" grow, I would have missed the sweet beauty they offered. Sometimes the buds growing in my yard were, in fact, weeds. But just as often, these were the buds before the blossom.

This is the lesson of the wildflowers. At first they don't look like flowers, they present as a weed. And if we fail to recognize them, we will miss their beauty. Sometimes what we most fear is just the bud before the blossom. If we are patient and let things unfold, we may discover an incredibly beautiful gift just waiting to be enjoyed. Other times, there was no blossom. It was just a weed as I suspected. The question is, when will we know? When should we pull the weeds? When should we let them grow? What happens if we pull too soon and miss the flower? What happens if we let it grow and the weeds get stronger and harder to pull up?

These are good questions about how to deal with fear, but ironically, they are questions born of fear. The fear of getting it wrong. The reality is we don't have to be afraid one way or the other. Here is a most wonderful thing about God. When we live with a sincere heart, God responds a lot like the wildflowers in my front yard. If I had pulled all the wildflowers and missed their bloom, amazingly they would come back again next year. They would give me another chance. In the same way, if we act on our fears too quickly and miss the message God has for us, the good news is that God is in the business of bringing new opportunities all the time. God is persistent in the giving of good gifts. Even if we flinch from the open hand of grace, mistaking it as an imminent slap, we are not disqualified from that grace. Grace just keeps on coming, gently, subtly, consistently. That is good news.

If we let the buds grow and they *were* just weeds, no blossom—no problem. That is when we pull the weeds. No punishment. Just a little work. The lesson is one of acceptance and trust that God is not out to trick us, but to offer us more freedom and love than we could ever exhaust.

God even wants to release us from our fear of misidentifying our fear.

This is the way grace works. If we accept it, it's ours to enjoy. If we miss it, it keeps coming back.

It's a free gift endlessly offered. When we're ready, the blossom will be there for us to enjoy. So a posture of hope, anticipation, and readiness is appropriate, not fear.

Whether we are confronted by some new idea about God, a new calling in life, a new relationship, or the end of something we love, we must let the words of Jesus resound in our hearts—"Take courage, it's me. Don't be afraid."

Sometimes the thing we fear the most is sent to free us.

THE CONSTANT GARDENER

Good News That Gets Better

After walking around the Louvre in Paris for more than an hour, I eventually found the *Mona Lisa* tucked away in what seemed like the basement. This painting got the special treatment. As I recall, it was encased in a thick glass box. I'm told the temperature and humidity were carefully monitored and controlled inside the case. Then there was a UV protective coating that kept flash photography from damaging it. There may have been some lasers involved or maybe that was a James Bond movie I'm remembering.

Nearby stood a large man in a blue blazer, hands clasped in fig-leaf formation, with requisite earpiece, name tag, and walkie-talkie. The security guard carefully scanned the crowd looking for suspicious behavior. Just his appearance made me feel guilty of a crime I wasn't planning to commit. I tried to act natural, which only made me act unnaturally.

Later I was visiting a botanical garden. While I walked the path I noticed a gardener pruning a tree. Perched perilously high on a ladder, she held a long pole in hand with a small saw attached to the end. The serrated blade threaded gently back and forth between some branches at the base of a limb. Special care was given not to nick the other branches as she worked to thin the canopy. Her relationship to the plants seemed to live somewhere between a mother tending a child and a sculptor molding clay.

Evidence of her care was also shown in the way saplings were protectively staked to the ground to keep them stable and growing in the right direction. Small plastic shields were wrapped around the base of some trees to protect the bark, presumably from a Weed Eater.

The gardener and the guard had two very different kinds of jobs. The guard's job was to protect and preserve ancient artifacts. The gardener's job was to cultivate and promote the growth of living things.

If the gardener treated her plants the way the guard treated the painting, the plants would most certainly die. Trees don't take kindly to small sealed glass cases that prevent moisture and the sun from getting in. An ancient painting would not take kindly to a whole lot of tampering, touch, and exposure. The key to selecting the proper method of care is understanding the object so the wrong methods are not applied.

The same is true when it comes to our relationship to the message of Jesus—the gospel. We must accurately understand the nature of the gospel if we are to treat it with proper care. I believe the *nature* of the gospel has often been misidentified.

A story in Acts 8 tells us about a disciple named Philip. He is sent by God on a two-day walk to a city that has been dead for a hundred years; an odd directive for someone wanting to share the good news with as many people as possible, since no one lived there.

Still, Philip obliges and along the way he encounters an Ethiopian eunuch riding in a chariot, reading aloud from the scroll of Isaiah. They strike up a conversation and the eunuch asks the meaning of the passage he is reading. Philip tells the eunuch that this passage is a prophecy foretelling the coming of Jesus. After a little more conversation, the eunuch asks, "What would prevent me from being baptized?" Apparently nothing, because Philip takes him to a nearby river and dunks him.

Immediately afterward Philip disappears; literally, he vanishes and is taken somewhere else, and the eunuch goes on his way.

This story is one of many conversion encounters in the book of Acts, but this one is special.

First, let me explain a little bit about eunuchs. There's no delicate way to put this: a eunuch is a man who has been castrated, sometimes voluntarily. Why would someone volunteer for such a gruesome procedure? In the ancient world there were a variety of reasons. In his case, it's because he was in the Nubian queen's service. Here's how it worked: If you wanted to serve the queen and you were male, you were required to become a eunuch as a way to protect the queen and empower her. Eunuchs didn't have the equipment to "cause trouble."

Some eunuchs would develop feminine characteristics because they no longer had as much testosterone coursing through their bodies. Many dressed in women's clothes with women's makeup and adornments, so they could serve powerful women without too many questions asked. They were considered a third gender and were often outcasts in society. People didn't know where to put them.

This particular eunuch was very interested in

the Jewish God. He traveled all the way from Africa to Jerusalem to worship, and he even acquired a scroll to take back with him, an act of courage since in Deuteronomy 23:1, the Bible strictly prohibits eunuchs from ever entering the assembly of God. He could worship and learn but he could never become part of the Jewish congregation. The reason is that to become a eunuch violates God's intended design and creative gift. A eunuch has willfully destroyed and disregarded God's gift of procreation.

God told Philip to go and share the gospel with a person who is not acceptable according to the Bible. He is from another land, another religion, and has chosen a lifestyle that is both irreversible and strictly prohibited in the Bible. And yet, God sends Philip far out of his way to share the good news with this person. Then Philip baptizes him without any precondition other than the eunuch's desire. So while the eunuch might be excluded from the religious assembly of God, he is welcome in God's kingdom.

Something else interesting is going on here. The eunuch, we are told, is carrying the scroll of Isaiah. This is not an accident; the book of Isaiah contradicts the law of Deuteronomy concerning eunuchs:

And let no eunuch complain,

"I am only a dry tree."

For this is what the LORD says:

"To the eunuchs who keep my Sabbaths,

who choose what pleases me

and hold fast to my covenant—

to them I will give within my temple and its walls

a memorial and a name

better than sons and daughters;

I will give them an everlasting name

that will endure forever. (Isaiah 56:3–5, NIV)

In Isaiah, God seems to change the rules of inclusion. God makes an adjustment from a covenant that includes a smaller number of people to a covenant that includes a larger number and more kinds of people.

This is the trajectory of the Bible as a whole. It is the story of an ever-expanding love that extends beyond the originally established boundaries. This is good news because unless you are Jewish you would have been excluded from the original covenant.

Another important part of the eunuch's story is not recorded in the Bible. Today, more than two thousand years after his conversion, over half of all Ethiopians are Christians, and a number of them trace the origin of their faith back to this first convert.

Here is a person utterly despised, feared, and outcast in ancient Jewish culture and religion. And not only did God welcome him into the kingdom, he also became the carrier and catalyst of the kingdom to a nation. God did all this without ever asking the eunuch to change anything about his life or lifestyle.

This "dry tree" was transformed into a seed. A seed that produced a vast forest that continues to yield fruit to this day.

It doesn't matter who you are, you are not excluded from this covenant of love and grace. You are not shut out from the assembly of God no matter what you've done, or what you've failed to do. You belong for one simple reason: God chooses to gift love.

The most challenging part of this reality is acceptance. Can we accept it? Or do we fight it, deny it, or doubt it? Can we be as courageous and faithful as this emasculated man? Can we accept the gift of transforming, healing, mending, restorative love? Will we receive love, especially when we feel we are least deserving of it?

Bring your authentic self to God—your worst. Bring whatever you've got to this God of love and you will find acceptance. God does not recoil from our dark corners. God is neither frightened nor angered by the skeletons hidden in our closets.

GARDENERS WANTED

According to Jesus, the reason he came into the world was to announce the good news. And the good news is this: The kingdom of God is at hand. In describing this kingdom he would often say "For those who have ears to hear..." before or after he would speak about it. He knew that not everyone would be ready for it. He talked about the kingdom more than anything else in his entire ministry, and he always spoke of it indirectly through metaphor, image, and story.

In chapter 13 of Luke's gospel, Jesus compares the kingdom of God to a mustard seed that someone planted in a field and it grew into a big tree so that the birds of the air could rest on its branches. For most of interpretive history, we have understood this to be a metaphor of numerical growth. That

God's kingdom will reach more people. I agree with this interpretation. But the metaphor may also be about the *nature* of the kingdom. A tree by its nature grows; it changes. Perhaps the nature of this kingdom is to grow, even change.

Perhaps the kingdom does more than transform us; it also transforms itself for our sake. There may be dimensions of God's love that have yet to be revealed to us. Just as God expanded the covenant to include an Ethiopian eunuch, as the world and conditions change today, it is possible that the gospel takes shapes necessary to better penetrate the hearts of people. A mustard seed in no way resembles the look, feel, or function of a mustard tree. This metaphor reflects perfectly the stark contrast in the message of God's love as traced from Deuteronomy through Isaiah to the book of Acts. The message of the gospel itself actually expands and includes more people and more kinds of people. Given the kingdom's tendency to grow, perhaps we should remain open and attentive to the unexpected shape it could take. In that sense the good news changes.

Like a seed that becomes a tree, it changes, grows, and is renewed in each culture, context, and generation. The good news began as a message to Abraham of the blessing of land and descendants for an ethnic group. But through the course of history it became the blessing of an abundant life beyond land and children, beyond ethnicity. It became good news for anyone who wanted it. Throughout scripture God's message is renewed, refocused, and expanded.

The good news grows and in that sense, changes.

And yet it stays the same. Its basic DNA does not change. It both changes and is somehow unchanged. The ever-changing gospel never changes. Regardless of new technology, complexity, and resources the world amasses or loses, no matter what our culture, creed, or skin color, the fundamental human longings never change.

Everyone, everywhere, at every time wants love, peace, freedom, and joy.

Because the most basic desire that begins with the first breath never changes, neither does what fulfills it. At the heart of the unchanging message is the promise that everyone who is thirsty has access to the Living Water. The unchanging good news is that peace is possible, love is unconditional, forgiveness is real, and grace is free. These never change.

Let's return to my experiences in the museum and the botanical garden for a moment. What if what Jesus said is actually true? What if the gospel is more like a plant than a painting? What if the gospel is more like a living organism than a lifeless artifact?

Some, in an effort to protect and preserve the gospel message, have become like the guards in that museum, fueled by fear that it could be damaged or stolen if they are not vigilant in their watch. They have mistaken the good news for an ancient artifact that needs to be protected. But that is not its nature. This kingdom is a lot more like a tree. God is looking for gardeners, not guards. A guard is trained in a defensive stance of fear and suspicion. A gardener is motivated by love and creativity.

What would it mean for us to position ourselves in a state of anticipation? The way a gardener might anticipate the unexpected reach and scope of new branches of a tree. Could we prepare ourselves to be surprised by the ways this kingdom reaches beyond its original boundaries to include more and more people, who were once thought justifiably excluded?

A friend, who is a landscape architect, once told me about a special kind of cell in plants that is called "meristematic." It's a cell that is

ever-growing,

ever-changing,

ever-living.

Jesus proclaimed the *meristematic* kingdom of God.

Are we prepared for this never-changing kingdom to change? Are we open to the ways we might understand it anew?

THE HIDDEN TREASURE

We Already Have What We Seek

A young landowner drove through Arizona on his move from the East Coast to California. He was so taken with the Sonoran Desert's natural beauty he decided to stay in Phoenix for a while.

As a land developer, he quickly saw potential for the natural beauty of the region to draw people. But after a little investigation with the locals he soon learned about a major barrier to building here—no water. Land was beautiful and cheap but with little access to water; building would be too cost prohibitive.

Some speculated that large underground water reservoirs existed beneath the surface of the desert floor and if you drilled deep enough and in the right places you might be able to find them—a risky and expensive undertaking.

The developer decided to take the risk. He hired a hydrologist and bought a parcel of land on his recommendation, found an experienced driller and began to dig. Days and weeks passed and there was no sign of water. The drill kept running.

Then one day the driller came to the developer and reported that they had found water. Without telling anyone he found water, the developer took nearly all the money he had and bought ten thousand acres of land in the area for a song. News of the water spread. Overnight, land values skyrocketed and he became a very wealthy man.

WHY JESUS CAME

In the book of Luke, chapter 4, verse 43, Jesus tells us the reason he came into the world: "I must proclaim the good news of the kingdom of God to the other cities also; for I was sent for this purpose." (NRSV)

Jesus was a teacher of ethics, an activist for justice, an agent of healing, a forgiver of sins, and the Messiah—anointed savior. But amid all these functions his actual stated purpose for coming into the world was to proclaim what he called "the kingdom of God."

The teachings of Jesus span a variety of topics. Sometimes he would take a side in existing religious debates about the law. Other times he talked about the age to come, our relationship to money and possessions, or issues of justice. But most of his time was spent teaching about the kingdom of God. This was very strange to his listeners because he wasn't talking about an existing religious idea. No reference to the phrase "kingdom of God" is made anywhere in the Old Testament or rabbinic writings. It is a completely fresh idiom introduced by Jesus.

The book of Matthew uses "the kingdom of *heaven*," which is a slightly different phrase to describe the same idea. This version of the phrase has caused many to assume that Jesus is talking about the place we go after we die. But that is not how Jesus talked about the kingdom of heaven. He most often talked about it as a present reality that has been here all along. He said, "The kingdom of heaven *is* at hand" (Matthew 10:7, ESV; italics added). He did not say, "It *will be* at hand."

Making matters more confusing, he didn't speak about this reality directly. Instead, he talked in parables and metaphors. He said, "The kingdom of heaven is like...

"...a mustard seed..."

"...a sower in a field..."

"...yeast in unleavened bread..."

"...a large net thrown into the sea..."

"...a merchant searching for pearls..."

And frequently he wouldn't explain what he meant. At one point the disciples even asked him why he spoke in parables all the time. Matthew 13:35 provides the answer: "This was to fulfill what was declared by the prophet when he said, 'I will open my mouth to speak in parables. I will declare what has been hidden from the foundation of the world.'" (ISV)

This explanation discloses part of a secret. The kingdom of God is not the announcement of something new, but rather shows us something very ancient. Jesus did not create it; he uncovered its existence. So, what is he revealing?

THE SECRET IS IN THE FIELD

One of the simplest parables of the kingdom goes like this, "The kingdom of heaven is like treasure hidden in a field. When a man found it, he hid it again, and then in his joy went and sold all he had and bought that field" (Matthew 13:44).

Interpreting parables is not always easy. They come with many layers. It's best to start simple. The most obvious meaning of this parable is that the kingdom of heaven is valuable. It is worth everything apparently. The man sold all he had to get it.

We also learn that the kingdom is somehow hidden, not entirely obvious to us. The treasure was hidden in a field.

Perhaps most importantly we learn that the kingdom produces joy. He sold all he had because of his joy. This is joy so powerful, so overwhelming, that it is worth more to you than any of your other attachments in life.

There is another, less obvious layer of meaning. The man finds a treasure and is thrilled with the discovery but what happens next is odd. He hides it again and goes and sells everything in order to buy the entire field.

Why not simply take the treasure he found? Why hide it again, sell everything he has, and buy the field? If he has the treasure, why does he need the field?

This is a very important detail. The parable is making a deliberate connection between the *field* and the *treasure*. And that is, they are inseparable. They are connected in the same way that the water reservoirs are locked in the desert land. The water the landowner wanted was impossible to claim without first owning the land. And the land is worthless without the water. The two are connected, inextricably linked just as in the parable of the treasure in the field.

The treasure is a symbol for the kingdom. Now, if the way to get the treasure is to first possess the field, it might be useful to know where to find the field.

TO REVEAL RATHER THAN CREATE

A clue can be found in an interaction Jesus has with the religious leaders of his day. At one point, they ask him a question. "Once, having been asked by the Pharisees when the kingdom of God would come, Jesus replied, 'The kingdom of God does not come with your careful observation, nor will people say, "Here it is," or "There it is," because the kingdom of God is within you'" (Luke 17:20–21).

Here we have the most important direct statement Jesus gives on the nature of this mysterious kingdom of God. From it we learn it is not something we will see on the outside. It will be experienced on the inside. The Pharisees were looking for signs and wonders, changes in politics, systems, and powers. But Jesus dismisses these, instead insisting the kingdom will not be found in things observed. Second, it is apparently not reserved for "believers." Jesus is speaking here to the Pharisees, those he had the most vehement disagreements with, the ones who were plotting to kill him. He called them "a brood of vipers." They are the very group for whom Jesus exhibited the least amount of grace. We might expect Jesus to tell his disciples that the kingdom is within them. But here he tells his most ardent critics, opponents, and enemies that the kingdom is found within them. This tells us something important about the message of the kingdom. Jesus did not say it only resides in the Pharisees. It's a statement of just how far reaching the kingdom is. If it resides in them, it can be found in anyone. Jesus is pointing to the most scandalous truth, one that no religion would appreciate, that the kingdom of heaven is within all of us.

Finally, Jesus says the kingdom is already here. Jesus is speaking in the present continuous verb tense, not the future tense. "The kingdom of God *is within you.*" He does not say, "The kingdom of God *will* be within you" or "*could* be within you" or "*might* be within you." He says it *is* within you.

So according to this passage, the kingdom of God is inside all of us now, not outside later. We are, in fact, the field. Each and every person on the planet. The treasure is in *us*. The dwelling place of God is in the last place we would ever expect to find it.

According to Jesus, the heaven we are waiting

for, the joy we long for, the peace we search for can be found hidden within us. This is easily overlooked, like the water reservoirs beneath the desert floor in Arizona, right under our feet. If we are looking for heaven, Jesus tells us we will not find it in things observed or out there somewhere. We will find it within.

The statement Jesus makes here is troubling for some. Even some Bible translators have tried to soften and misdirect the meaning of this passage by rendering it "The kingdom of heaven is *among* you." This version makes the meaning more opaque and vague, but it's designed to make it less self-focused. These translators locate heaven outside us somewhere, like a cloud in the sky. They don't tell us exactly where though.

The Greek word that is being translated as *among* is the word "*entos*." However, the word doesn't mean *among*. The meaning is made clear when Jesus uses it in Matthew 23:26. In this passage, Jesus instructs the Pharisees that they must "clean the inside [*entos*] of the cup." The meaning here, as well as in the Luke passage, is clearly *inside* or *within*.

Jesus expresses the same notion in the book of John. In John's gospel he uses phrases like "living water" or "eternal life" instead of "kingdom of heaven." But he is describing the same reality. At one point he stands before a large crowd at a festival and says, "Whoever believes in me, as the Scripture has said, streams of living water will flow from within him" (John 7:38). Notice the words here. We might expect Jesus to say something like "The streams of water will flow *from God to him.*" Instead he says, "Living water will flow *from within him.*"

It is common in religious Christianity for people to be taught to prefer certain parts of the Bible that emphasize our fundamental emptiness, our depravity, and the subsequent need for God to pour into us. Scripture does sometimes use this metaphor to describe what God does. Paul, the writer of much of the New Testament, quite likes such metaphors.

But in the above passage, Jesus describes it differently. He says we already have what we need, we just can't seem to see it without his help. Just because the kingdom is in us doesn't mean we automatically experience it. The landowner needed help to get the water. Jesus is like the hydrologist, who knows where to look for the water and has the tools to drill.

Jesus functions like a mirror. I have a face, but I can't see it without a mirror. The mirror doesn't give me a face; it only shows me what I already have. Jesus describes what he does as showing us what we already have. He reveals rather than creates.

THE DAY WE ARE BORN, IT BEGINS

In John's gospel, when he speaks to the woman at the well, he says, "But whoever drinks the water I give them will never thirst. Indeed, the water I give them will become in them a spring of water welling up to eternal life" (John 4:14, NIV).

The phrase "eternal life" is almost always understood as a synonym for heaven after we die. But that is not how Jesus uses this phrase. Jesus says that eternal life is "welling up" or "springing up." This is a very specific construction of a Greek verb. As in English, a Greek verb can be constructed in a particular way to convey different aspects of meaning. It could be a future tense, or a one-time event (i.e., "she will run"). But in this case, the verb tense is actually a present participle (i.e., "she is running"). The action is occurring and continuing in the present moment, not a one-time event somewhere in the future. Eternal life is a possibility here and now, not just there and then. We can experience boundless joy, indestructible love, and abiding peace while we live.

The possibility of eternal life begins the day we are born, not the day we die.

Paul expresses the same truth using a different metaphor. In his first letter to the church in the city of Corinth he writes, "Do you not know that your bodies are temples of the Holy Spirit?" (6:19, NIV). The dwelling place of the Divine is *you*. And it's happening right now.

The body that carries us through life also carries the Divine.

This incredibly simple, direct, and profound teaching has been very difficult for many to accept. The Christian religion has conditioned us to believe that heaven is something we only experience after we die, and it is a place we go. But Jesus teaches that heaven is available now, within us. Christianity has long emphasized only one song from the Bible, which is we are wretched sinners—"by nature objects of wrath" (Ephesians 2:3). So it's hard to imagine anything this good residing inside us.

The notion that the Divine dwells inside us may sound fuzzy or even New Age-y or provoke fears that this understanding leads to narcissistic navel gazing and self-centered living. It is not a dangerous teaching and will not cause us to worship ourselves instead of God. That occurs only when we confuse the container with the content. Just because we carry the Divine does not mean *we* are Divine. A clay bowl is a clay bowl. It may be worth a few dollars. If you fill that bowl with gold, it doesn't change the nature of the bowl. But, as long as the gold is in the bowl, the bowl becomes as valuable as the gold. As soon as the gold is poured out, the value of the bowl returns to that of a bowl. As long as we live, we are like clay pots filled to the brim with gold. As long as the breath visits this body, we are no less than God carriers—containers of the Divine. And the content we carry will continue long after our bowl breaks.

This is a simple observation of reality. The notion that we carry something of exquisite value and power is something intrinsic to the human experience. We have been given a unique capacity that never deteriorates.

My father is eighty-four years old. His hearing is not so good, his eyesight is dim, his balance is going, his body isn't as strong as it once was, his memory is fading rapidly, and he is easily confused. This is the natural part of the aging process—the body and mind are deteriorating. For all of us, this is the story of life. The moment we are born, with the first breath, the decay begins.

But something in my father is undiminished. It is as strong as it ever was and shows no signs of fading. His capacity to love is as strong as ever. His ability to enjoy beauty and friendship is undiminished. His appreciation of joy and the ability to be grateful is no less than when he was young. Inside him resides a capacity for joy, love, gratitude, and appreciation that never fades.

Something inside us does not diminish even when our body and mind deteriorate. Perhaps this is part of what Jesus meant when he said the kingdom of God is within you. Where do the love, joy, peace, and gratitude we experience come from? Are these not the qualities of the kingdom? This is not to say they don't manifest themselves outside us. They do, but according to Jesus, the kingdom—an experience of unwavering joy—begins within us and may find expression in the world through us.

TWO KINDS OF JOY

Two different kinds of joy exist. And they are often easily mistaken for each other. One kind of joy comes from the world outside, and another joy comes from a place inside. The inner joy is completely independent of everything else that happens in life. It is easy to confuse the joy on the inside with the joy that comes from the outside, especially when so many things outside us give us joy.

To see the difference, consider what happens when you lose a loved one. The person you love is no longer around, the object of affection is gone. But remarkably, the love you have for that person remains, it persists. You can still access and feel love for the person who is no longer with you.

This is because the experience of love is located within you, not in the other person. You can feel love for another whether they are in the same room or on the other side of the world or have since passed away. In the same way, the joy, peace, and power of the kingdom of heaven are found inside us, not outside. This joy is unwavering and is independent of what happens in the outside world. Jesus came to help us access, uncover, and connect to this kingdom within.

Hidden in the field of our body and being is the greatest treasure the world has ever known. At the moment of birth we were given a lease on some incredibly valuable land—a body to experience life with. We don't own the land, eventually the lease comes up and the body returns to the dust. But if we find the treasure hidden inside it now, then we can keep it for eternity.

One of the most overlooked messages of the kingdom is that we already have what we seek. There is nothing standing between us and the river we long to find. We must simply learn what is required to access it.

For Jesus it begins with uncovering our *thirst*.

A CONNOISSEUR OF WINE

The Power of Thirst

A wine connoisseur doesn't drink wine because she is thirsty. She drinks wine because she enjoys the intricate flavors. She is concerned with the ritual leading up to the pouring. She is interested in the proper container and how to hold her glass in the appropriate way. Red wine is served at room temperature and can be held by the bulb of the glass, but white wine is served chilled and should be held by the stem so the warmth of her fingers doesn't prematurely raise the temperature of the beverage.

A connoisseur is one who develops a certain kind of expertise. Expertise meaning the ability to make distinctions. The more you learn about a subject, skill, or art, the better able you are to make distinctions. At first you learn the gross distinctions like the difference between red and white wines. Then you learn the difference between a Merlot and a Shiraz. Then you learn the different types of Shiraz. You start examining the chemical makeup of the beverage, the region, the year, the kind of grapes used, or whether it has "legs" (how much it sticks to the glass when you swirl it around). You look at the type of wood the storage barrel is made of. You start grasping a new language to further those distinctions. Words and phrases like "smoky," "velvety," "fruit forward," "long finish," "full-bodied spice," and "masked by a hint of oak" become meaningful. You begin to understand the ingredients just by inspecting the bouquet of the wine. You start using phrases like "inspecting the bouquet" instead of "smelling." This is what mastery is all about.

Religious people have a habit of developing a similar relationship to their doctrine and beliefs. Over time, many become connoisseurs of their religion. People who learn to appreciate and make subtle distinctions develop a refined sense of what kind of behavior and belief are okay and not okay. They develop an interest in detecting the subtlest of theological distinctions and nuance. They prefer to congregate and associate with other people who like the same kinds of doctrines and dogmas.

Nothing is wrong with developing a mastery of religion. The problem is that mastery of our religion has almost nothing to do with Jesus and what he came to do in the world.

When Jesus stands before the festival crowd in John 7 and announces that streams of Living Water will flow from within us, he reveals an important caveat, a preface. This gift of eternal life is only a *possibility* for people, not a certainty. It comes with a condition. In John 7:37 Jesus begins his proclamation by saying: "*If anyone is thirsty*, let him come to me and drink." (emphasis added)

The first condition is simply to be *thirsty*. What Jesus offers may be for anyone, but it is not for everyone. The experience of eternal life is exclusively reserved for thirsty people. It's available to anyone, but not everyone will choose it. I have running water in my house at all times. But unless I'm thirsty, I won't drink it. If we want to have eternal life now, it begins by experiencing the thirst for that Living Water.

The thirst is the quest, the fundamental human longing for peace, fulfillment, love, and joy. Some call it the search for meaning, the search to find God, or our reason for being here. Whatever you call it, they all lead back to the basic longing for peace, joy, and love. The quest is common to every human who ever lived. It drives many of our choices in life. We get married, make love, have children, quit our jobs and find new ones, buy homes, and go on vacation, all in search of joy. Some of us are more or less aware of this quest at different times. But it is the intensity of that longing that drives the search.

We must become slaves of that intensity to get what we truly want.

This is what makes the interaction between Jesus and the woman at the well so interesting. After a brief conversation where Jesus reveals to her the Living Water that could flow from within her, she says, "Sir, give me this water so that I won't get thirsty and have to keep coming here to draw water" (John 4:15).

This seems like a simple enough and straightforward request. But Jesus takes the conversation in a very strange and unexpected direction.

> He told her, "Go, call your husband and come back."
>
> "I have no husband," she replied.
>
> Jesus said to her, "You are right when you say you have no husband. The fact is, you have had five husbands, and the man you now have is not your husband. What you have just said is quite true." (John 4:16–18)

This is a surprising turn in the story. We might expect Jesus to say something like "Repent of your sin and believe in me and you will have that water." But he doesn't say this. Instead he makes a simple observation about her life without even a hint of judgment. He doesn't call it sin, nor does he tell her to change the way she is living. Jesus merely reflects back to her the strategies she has used to make it in life. He's making a point here.

Growing up I used to play T-ball. And after every game a different family would rotate who would bring the drinks for after the game. I vividly remember the assortment of carbonated beverages we could choose from. It was a thrilling reward for us but there was only one problem. These drinks contain caffeine, sodium, or sugar, three ingredients that actually work to dehydrate your body. Coke works to mask our thirst rather than actually quenching it. Wine works the same way. It contains alcohol, which is a contaminant to the thirst-quenching properties of the water.

One of the things Jesus is up to here is pointing out the strategy the woman is using to mask her own thirst. He is showing her how this string of relationships, whatever the reason for them, may function like Coke. It actually dehydrates her while at the same time hiding from her just how thirsty she really is. In answer to her question, Jesus is actually saying: Do you notice what you've done in life to make sure you don't feel thirsty? These choices temporarily cover over your longing. Don't be afraid of your desire for more. Welcome it, and it will drive you to find the true water and the One who can show it to you. Feel your desire for this water, that longing for more in your life, the quest to be fulfilled, at peace, in love, and at home. One way to do that is to become aware of the counterfeit ways you currently attempt to quench the thirst.

There is a very simple requirement to accessing this river—you must be thirsty. If you aren't thirsty, it isn't for you.

Our world presents us with abundant distractions that dull the pang of our thirst but do nothing to quench it. Things like illicit drug use and sexual immorality we generally consider "bad." But far more common and perhaps bigger barriers are things we call "good." Nearly everything we do in life is an effort to quench our fundamental thirst. We seek intimate relationships, have children, pursue meaningful work, serve the poor. We try to make more money, spend more money, give more money away. We look for it in food or in the achievement of personal success.

None of these things are wrong. The only downside is that they all eventually change and disappear. The joy derived from and attached to these things is fleeting. If these are our only sources of joy, we will be thirsty again. The water Jesus promises is not dependent on any of them, or on life going the way we want. The joy he points to and offers is independent, unending, unchanging, and immovable.

THE THIRSTY DON'T CARE ABOUT THE CUP

Jesus doesn't condemn the woman at the well for having multiple men in her life. He only holds up a mirror to help her see what she already knows is a problem. Jesus in effect says, "You can do that if you want. But I want to show you something more. I actually want to show you something that can quench your thirst any time you want it. A kind of water that does not depend on the security a husband provides, or his affection and admiration.

This water is available to you whenever you need it. It travels with you, because it is within you at all times. If you are thirsty, then drink from the well within. I will show you."

When I was in seminary I was immersed in the intellectual aspects of the Christian faith. This was a place of rigorous training for academic accreditation. And we were taught an entirely new language pattern where words were created to further parse, divide, and subdivide the distinctions between other ideas. The more books I read that described the differences between theological positions and biblical interpretations, the more I argued and debated. I developed a growing certainty that these distinctions really were matters of the utmost importance. I became a connoisseur of my religion.

But that sense of importance in the distinctions slowly disappeared when I started serving as a hospital chaplain in Los Angeles. I walked into the room of a fifty-five-year-old woman, a Russian Jew, who had been mugged and shot in the stomach and lived to tell about it. My finely honed theological abstractions about *the-penal-substitutionary-theory-of-the-atonement* had nothing to say in the face of a woman suffering such physical and psychological trauma. All she wanted was healing, peace, and hope. She was thirsty.

Then there was the Independent Fundamentalist Baptist pastor who made Jerry Falwell look like a godless liberal. His wife had an obstructed bowel and they didn't know why. A week later we learned she had cancer and two months to live. The course of our conversations over the weeks that followed focused on the precious gift of life and how much he loved her. Our theological differences simply lost their relevance. He was simply thirsty.

What became important was the expression of love and the sudden need to savor and appreciate every last ounce of existence. In their humble state of exquisite need, they found the sweet water of life that Jesus promised. It didn't come in the form of doctrines, beliefs, proclamations, or rituals. It came in the stillness of the heart now able to see the gift they always already had.

I met liberals, fundamentalists, Unitarians, atheists, Muslims, Jews, gays, good fathers and bad fathers, divorced people and those happily married, those who had affairs and those who were faithful, the overeducated and undereducated, the mean-spirited and bitter, and those who were kind. The refined theological, religious judgments I had in my head dissolved in the face of people who longed for peace, healing, joy, and love.

One kind of joy comes from wine, the other comes from water. Wine is good as long as we know what it's for. It's not so helpful when we use it for a purpose for which it wasn't intended. Wine was not designed to quench our thirst. If we use it for that reason, we will be very disappointed and drunk. Thirsty people don't go looking for wine varietals. They don't ask what year or region it comes from or care about the shape of the glass. Instead, they just want water, however it comes.

This thirst is the great equalizer. It doesn't matter how rich we are because no amount of money can buy this water. It doesn't matter how holy or sinful we are. The water makes no judgments. This water is here even when we aren't thirsty, nor is it offended if we don't want it. The point of the thirst is simply to drive us to find the water.

When we are truly thirsty, we don't care what kind of container the water comes in and we will ignore appropriate etiquette. All other beverages will pale in comparison to this pristine Living Water.

When we are thirsty, we are no longer interested in that which divides us, but rather that which joins us. The common need, we all need water. We all need joy and peace in our lives, that river of Living Water offered endlessly in every moment of our existence.

WAVES ON THE OCEAN

Two Kinds of Life

John 12:25 usually reads as a paradox: "The man who loves his life will lose it, while the man who hates his life in this world will keep it for eternal life." The Bible has a number of these apparent contradictions: In weakness we are made strong (see 2 Corinthians 12:10). Only in dying will we truly live (see John 12:24). It is in giving that we might receive (see Acts 20:35). We must become humble in order to be lifted up (see James 4:10).

The verse in John looks like an impossibility but when read more carefully, it's a tragedy. If I love my life I will lose it, but if I hate it I get to keep it. Neither is a good deal. Either way I'm out of luck. I don't get what I love. I don't want to keep what I hate. This is not a paradox, it's a bummer.

But another layer of meaning is hidden in the original language. Jesus distinguishes between two different kinds of "life" in this passage; we just don't see it in the English translation. In this verse Jesus uses two distinct words that are each translated as *life*. One is "*psyche*" and the other is "*zoe*."

"The man who loves his life [*psyche*] will lose it, while the man who hates his life [*psyche*] in this world will keep it for eternal life [*zoe*]."

If we have a strong attachment to *psyche* we will lose it. But if we shed our attachments to it, we will gain it as well as something Jesus called *zoe*.

The Greek word "*psyche*" is sometimes translated as *soul*. Which is where we get the word "psychology"—the study of the soul. It also broadly means *life*. Specifically it refers to all things that make up a person's life. In the context of this passage, our *psyche* is what comprises our ego, personality, relationships, possessions, and achievements. That's one aspect of our life. You might call this your "personal life."

When Jesus uses the word "*psyche*" it is in reference to something that was created, can be lost, and one day will pass away. This kind of life is set within time and has a beginning and an end. In John 10:11, Jesus says, "I am the good shepherd. The good shepherd lays down his life [*psyche*] for the sheep."

When Jesus laid down his "life" on the cross he lost his *psyche*, not his *zoe*. Everything that happens *in* our life is the *psyche*. And one day it will come to an end one way or another. That is the nature of the *psyche* life. It's temporary.

The other word for life is "*zoe*," which refers to something else. In the opening of John's Gospel he uses this word to describe Jesus. "In him was life [*zoe*], and that life [*zoe*] was the light of all people" (John 1:4, NRSV).

This word shows up a lot in John's writings on the lips of Jesus, especially where he applies it to us. It is almost always paired with the adjective "*aeon*." *Aeon* often translates into *eternal* or *everlasting*. Jesus came to show us *aeon zoe*—eternal life.

Aeon has two primary meanings. It can refer to a season or era with a beginning and an end. But far more often it refers to an experience that resides *outside of time*. And because it exists outside of time, it has no beginning or end. In one sense *aeon zoe* has no birth or death date. When we say the word "forever" we mean an endless succession of seconds, minutes, and hours unfolding in linear sequence. But that is not the tone of this word. When the ancients used the word "*aeon*" it was about the fullness of an experience that has no relationship to time. To try and equate the two would be a bit like asking, How fast is the color blue? The categories don't equate to one another.

The distinction between these two kinds of life—*psyche* (what happens *in* our life) and *zoe* (existence itself)—is a tricky one. It's easy to confuse the two and blur the line between them. A few analogies might help.

Consider the weather. Storms rage and then they disappear. Clouds come and then they go. Weather, by nature, constantly changes. It can be beautiful and terrifying, sometimes all at once. The weather is like *psyche*; things that happen to us in our life. They come and go, rise and fall. But the boundless, immovable sky contains all of this weather. It is easily missed amid the spectacle of the weather. The sky is untouched and unaffected by what happens within it. *Zoe* is like the sky.

Or think about the ocean. Some days it is calm and serene, other days it is tumultuous. The *psyche* is like the surface of the ocean. Sometimes the waves are crashing and dangerous, like when you lose a job, or someone says they hate you and can't forgive you, or someone you love goes away. Other days the waves are rolling and gentle, even peaceful, as in instances when your family is close and happy, when your career is going the way you want and your bank account and belly are full. Beneath the surface of the ocean, in the depths, is a place that is not a slave to the elements. It could be World

War III on the surface, but down below in the deep places is another realm, like a womb, untouched by all that is happening on the surface. That undersea expanse is the *zoe*.

The *psyche* is the life we are confronted with every time we open our eyes. Everything we can see out there is the *psyche*. According to Jesus, the *zoe* is not seen with the eyes, but experienced inside.

Imagine a sunrise that bathes the whole earth in radiant and glorious light. Then imagine you took the most incredible picture of it. The reds are brighter and more spectacular than in real life. It's almost hyper-real—we're talking screen-saver awesome.

Now, should you ever find yourself in a dark room in need of light, you will discover that, no matter how brilliantly the photograph captured the sun, it is utterly useless. The picture is beautiful, but a firefly can produce more light than that image. The picture is our *psyche*. It is beautiful and should be enjoyed. But by its nature cannot produce the light we need. *Zoe* is the sun, the source of the light we most long for.

If *psyche* is what happens in our life, *zoe* is life itself, like the breath that enters us. No matter what happens in our *psyche*, *zoe* is faithful, always there no matter what. A constant companion that never judges. It never feels slighted, it accepts being rejected and ignored and still dispenses the gift effortlessly. It has no need to punish when we forget and ignore it. *Zoe* goes by many names. Some call it "unconditional love," others use the word "grace," still others name it a "peace that passes understanding."

We often look to our *psyche* for the things only *zoe* can provide—permanent peace, constant joy, unconditional love. But this is not the nature of the *psyche*. It is highly conditional, always moving, ever-changing. Our ability to distinguish between the two kinds of life is crucial. When we erase the distinction in our minds, we experience great disappointment when things don't go the way we wish. When we lose this precarious difference, we suffer greatly. It takes continual effort to see it clearly moment to moment. To live from *zoe* requires daily practice, and that is why it is revealed in the Bible as only a possibility, not a certainty. The reason it is only a possibility is because it depends on us. We have a choice before us in every moment.

With this distinction in mind, we understand the verse that opened this chapter as Jesus presenting a choice between the two ways of life. We can either choose the way of *psyche* or the way of *zoe*.

However, this choice is not simply binary, one or the other. It is a matter of sequence.

A teacher once explained it as the relationship between ones and zeros. The value of zero and one is determined entirely by their sequence. If you put a zero in front of a one, it does not change the value of the one. If you put three zeros before a one, it does not change the value of the one. You could put a million zeros in front of the one and it does not change the value of the one. The value of the one will stay a one. Likewise, the value of the zero will remain zero in all these instances.

However, if you place the one in front of the zero, suddenly you have ten, add three zeros after the one and it's a thousand. As long as the one is placed first, every zero you add increases the value of the one and the zero. Get the sequence right and the value of both is transformed in powerful ways.

Zoe is a one, *psyche* is a zero. Get them out of order and you lose the value. Get them in the right order and you become rich beyond measure. Jesus said this another way in Matthew 6:33, "seek first his kingdom . . . and all these things will be given to you as well."

According to Jesus, one of the main reasons we don't experience and enjoy the power of *eternal life* now is that we have our priorities out of order. We are caught up and distracted by the spectacle of *psyche* life and the challenge of managing, building, creating, and recreating our life and lifestyles. Our responsibilities and our wishes often take first priority. God is not opposed to those other things. He created the world and called it good. But God does repeatedly stress the danger of getting it all in the right order of importance.

The Old Testament uses the word "idolatry" to describe this problem. The first commandment is, "You shall have no other gods *before me*." Notice this is about sequence, getting the order right. God doesn't say you shall have no other gods—period. Whether we know it or not, God seems to know we will have other gods. The important thing is that they are not prioritized before God. I don't use the word "gods" as a reference to mythological figures or statues we worship (though that happens too). Instead, whatever we become attached to or fall in love with has the potential to become a god in our mind. It could be food, our computer, our spouse, or even our kids.

God is the Creator and everything God created has the potential to become a substitute god for us. The problem is when the created comes *before* the Creator—not because it offends God. We humans have an amusing trait. We often assume that because we were created in God's image that God is a lot like a human. We often project onto God our own human characteristics—like unmet needs around recognition and praise. But God doesn't share these traits of ours. We do not honor God *first* for God's sake, as if our recognition somehow props up God's sense of self. The reason God warns us about idolatry is because it hurts us, not God. It distracts us from the true source of the Living Water.

Jesus presents us with two kinds of life: The way of *psyche*—a life encased in time and destined to die, marked by the churning waves of rise and fall, health and sickness, gain and loss, joy and pain. And the way of *zoe*—a life that has no birth or death date, one that does not fail us or leave us, but one that endures in endless radiance and simple serenity.

Just because *psyche* is fleeting and fickle, and *zoe* is eternal and immovable, it would be easy to mistake one as a curse and the other a grace. But these two kinds of life are both inestimable gifts. Understanding the difference and appreciating them in the right order makes their value apparent.

Get them in the wrong sequence and we will have missed the point of our entire existence. But if we place the *one* before the *zero*, the Creator before the created, we will find the river and experience blessings beyond our wildest dreams.

THE DUNE IS HEAVY

One Who Lightens the Load

If what Jesus said is true, that what we are looking for is within us, it raises an important question. Some might even find it disturbing. If I already have what I want, why do I or anyone need Jesus?

There is the simple and most obvious answer—he's the one who told us about it. Without him we wouldn't know. Then there is the slightly more interesting answer, which I mentioned in the previous chapter: A face is something we already have, but we cannot see it without a mirror. Among his many roles, Jesus acts as a mirror that shows us who we really are and what we really have.

The reasons above are true, but in a more significant way, Jesus is important because of who he is. In the first letter of John it says "This is how God showed his love among us: He sent his one and only Son into the world that we might live through him. This is love: not that we loved God, but that he loved us and sent his Son as an atoning sacrifice for our sins" (1 John 4:9–10).

In this passage John tells us a couple of very

important things about both the nature and function of Jesus. Concerning his nature, John tells us that Jesus is the "one and only" Son of God.

The New American Standard Bible renders it "God has sent His *only begotten* Son into the world" (emphasis added). This is a phrase John has used before in his Gospel. John 3:16 says "God so loved the world, that He gave His *only begotten* Son" (emphasis added).

The notion that Jesus is *the* Son of God is an important one in Christianity. While I affirm this, I also acknowledge the places in scripture that suggest that anyone can become a son or daughter of God (John 1:12, Acts 17:29, Luke 20:36, Galatians 3:26).

This apparent contradiction is a function of the translation. In the passages translated *only begotten*, the original Greek word is "*monogene.*" "God sent his *monogene* son." The word is comprised of two Greek words: "*mono*" meaning *one*, and "*gene*," which means *kind*. Jesus is "one of a kind," which carries the meaning of *unique* rather than *only*. The International Standard Version rightly translates it as "He gave his *unique* Son…into the world" (emphasis added). Perhaps this distinction seems insignificant. But there is a difference between being the "only" son and a "unique" son. The implications are important.

My grandmother makes an incredible sweet tea. It is a pleasure I only get to enjoy a few times a year when I visit her. At one point, I decided I must have this tea in my life on a more regular basis. So I asked her for the recipe and made it for myself. Oddly, it didn't work. I realized I had used a different brand of tea and sweetener, so I corrected this error only to discover the tea still didn't taste like hers. It was somehow slightly off. Eventually I even got to the point of superstition and bought the same kind of container she used, as though the shape held the key to its taste. It did not.

Finally I thought perhaps I remembered the taste wrong. Maybe I inflated it in my imagination. The next time I returned, I was eager to try her tea. It was as spectacular as I remembered!

When I made the tea, everything was right, the proportions exact, the ingredients a match, even the proper container. But it didn't taste like my grandmother's tea. The only way for me to get my grandmother's tea is from my grandmother. Most likely, it is something in her water. Whatever the reason, my grandma provides some ingredient that I can only get when I'm there with her. In this sense, it is unique, one of a kind.

Now, I can find tea in lots of places; I'm not denied access to beverages. In the same way you can find a son or daughter of God on every street corner. We are all children of God. But there was one son who was one of a kind. Among all the children of God, this one is unique, not only in who he was, but also in what he could do.

NO MORE SUBSTITUTES

The most commonly understood function of Jesus is that he forgives sin, which gives us access to God. John uses the phrase "atoning sacrifice" to describe this. This is actually a metaphor that points to a particular aspect of the ancient worldview that we no longer hold. There was once a belief that anything you've done wrong in your life could be undone, or atoned, by the ritual killing of an animal. For us this is extremely bizarre, crude, and superstitious. It's based on the assumption that the gods had to use up a certain amount of wrath. So people started using decoys or substitutes to deflect the wrath. Instead of pouring out wrath on me, if I present God with a goat, God applies the wrath to the goat. How clever, problem solved, wrath avoided, sin forgiven, and God is none the wiser.

The length of suspension from the wrath was

usually dependent on the size of your animal. A small bird might only get you a couple of weeks, a big beautiful cow maybe a whole year.

Once the allotted time period expired, you'd have to go back and do it again to avoid the wrath. This is the context of the metaphor John presents and by using the metaphor John is actually critiquing that worldview. In a way he says "Hey, you know how people are always sacrificing goats so God doesn't get mad at them? Well, imagine for a moment that Jesus is like that goat, he took on our sin. The only difference is he did it once and for all. So that whole substitutionary atonement thing isn't really necessary anymore."

We don't actually practice substitutionary punishment in our culture. So this metaphor isn't as helpful. Other metaphors work better for us. For instance, if you have accrued a huge credit card debt and the company comes along and simply says "Hey, don't worry about it, your debt has been completely absolved just because we felt like it." Imagine how good that would feel. Imagine the freedom of a yoke like that lifted off your shoulders. The point of these and other metaphors about what Jesus did is to hint at the effect Jesus had, rather than to attempt to detail a specific mechanism. These are not about how God works; they are about what it feels like to receive the gift of God. God is nothing like a credit card company. The metaphor doesn't describe how God works, but rather the freedom one might feel after having been forgiven a huge financial debt. That is what it feels like to taste God's grace.

This "substitutionary" metaphor and function of Jesus is the one most people are quite familiar with. For some reason this is the one function of Jesus that religious Christianity is most excited about. Admittedly, of all his gifts, this is the one I'm least eager to receive, simply because in order to get this gift, I have to die first.

Jesus had another function as well. This is the second aspect that makes Jesus so unique. It's also the one most often overlooked in religious Christianity—one we get to experience while we are alive. And yet it's the one John mentions first. It takes primacy.

Verse 9 of John's gospel says, "God sent his unique son that we might *live through him*." Before we get to the part about atoning for sin after we die, we are shown a gift while we live. Jesus came so that we might live through him, not just die with him. This is where things get interesting.

A VICARIOUS CLIMB

In an area on the eastern shore of Lake Michigan sits an astounding geological formation. Millions of years of wind, water, ice, and rain have pulverized rock into piles of sand, leaving behind enormous four-hundred-foot-high dunes. This region has been turned into a state park so people can climb, camp, and recreate in them.

One day we were visiting and my youngest daughter, who was three at the time, decided she wanted to hike too. I was amazed at her tenacity. I held her hand as we began the climb. Each step, our feet sank into the sand, leaving our steps without purchase or noticeable progress. It can be quite disheartening at first, like walking up a down escalator. When you reach the top, you've only ascended a few hundred feet in terms of altitude, but you've hiked what feels like a thousand to get there. What makes the frustration worthwhile isn't the view, it's the thrill of sprinting down a giant steep sand dune and crashing along the way without injury—just the soft embrace of the finest white sand.

As we labored up the steep incline, my daughter looked up at me and said, "Dad, this dune is heavy."

It took me a minute to register what she was saying. "You mean, this is a hard climb?"

She said, "Yes, the dune is heavy" and kept repeating it throughout the hike, which made me chuckle. I agreed with her each time.

When I could tell she was starting to tire, and to avoid the tantrum phase of the climb, I asked, "Do you want me to carry you on my shoulders?"

She stopped and gave me a look of betrayal as if to say *You mean to tell me we could have been doing that the whole time?* "Yes, put me on your shoulders!" she said.

There was still a long way to go, so I carried her the rest of the way up. The dune got a "little heavier" the moment she perched on my shoulders. I didn't mind. It was one of those moments of recognition. I will not always be able to carry her on my shoulders. I relished it. As she rode on my shoulders, this thought occurred to me: She was hiking the dune *through* me.

To *live through* Jesus is to be in relationship with him. He is there to do the heavy lifting for us, to insulate us from the elements and resistance, so that we can engage them with resilience, kindness, gratitude, and hope. It is tempting to try and hike this dune of life on our own. But someone much stronger than us is eager to help. He will never force us to get on his shoulders. It begins with our own humble request. "I need some help, this dune is way too heavy for me." This is a choice we make, not once and for all, but on a moment-by-moment basis. Even if you've been hiking on your own for a very long time, in an instant he can lift you up and place you on strong and easy shoulders. He even seems to enjoy it. This capacity and power is what makes Jesus truly unique among all God's sons and daughters. He has the ability to connect us to the great insulator, that which we already have—the kingdom of God within, where streams of Living Water quench our deepest thirst.

When we make that choice and experience the relief, it is a taste of eternal life.

MORE THAN A NAME

Despite his incredible power and limitless capacity, Jesus has an unusual trait. He is exceptionally humble. So humble, in fact, he often didn't need to be acknowledged for what he did. Sometimes he would even say things like "Don't tell anyone who I am" (see Mark 1:43–44 and 8:29–30).

The implication of this kind of humility is often

ignored among religious Christians. Christians are quite insistent on the need to call upon the name of Jesus for salvation. But here the grace of God extends even further than we imagine. Jesus can lift us up even when we fail to ask or don't know his name. This is perhaps one of the most difficult concepts for religious Christians to accept. That Jesus can do his work independent of us or even without his name being proclaimed.

A great deal of attention in the Bible is given to the importance of using and proclaiming the "name" of Jesus (Matthew 24:4; Mark 6:14 and 9:39; Luke 1:31; John 20:31; throughout Acts, Ephesians, Philippians, Colossians, 2 Thessalonians, and the list goes on). I affirm the beauty and power of Jesus' name. I believe knowing the exact address of your destination can help you get there faster.

However, many religious Christians have become so enamored of the "name" they have come to believe that the name itself, the phonetic sounds, or written letters are invested with magical power. As if this is a token we can deposit into the vending machine of God to get what we wish for. With our focus so squarely placed on the name, we can easily miss what the name refers to. The true power is derived not from the name, but from the power behind it. That power is not bound by a name.

Jesus confronts this possibility in religious people when he says in Matthew 7:22–23, "Many will say to me in that day, 'Lord, Lord, did we not prophesy in your name, and in your name drive out demons and perform many miracles?' Then I will tell them plainly, 'I never knew you.'"

It is the person, not the name, that possesses the power. A parrot can repeat the name of Jesus but that doesn't mean it can evoke his power.

One of the greatest problems with this worship of the name rather than the person is that it diminishes the power of Christ. We may begin to assume that the power of Jesus cannot exist apart from his name. As if without his name being called he is not capable of acting. We begin to act as though Jesus is at our disposal and that we can withhold him or deploy him as we see fit and he will be obedient to our whims.

THE ANONYMOUS DONOR

As I walked a brick pathway of the botanical garden I noticed many of the bricks had names etched in them—they were honoring donors. Casually taking in the various names in the unlikely event I knew someone, I stopped on a particular brick that had an odd inscription. It simply said "anonymous." Someone gave money and withheld his or her name. The garden decided to print it anyway, acknowledging that someone, somewhere made a donation.

Anonymous donations are not uncommon. Hundreds of millions of dollars are given anonymously every year to charities and educational institutions. The reasons for this are many. Not least of which is some people don't need credit to make an impact on the world. They prefer to do it for their own enjoyment instead of for recognition.

If we who are merely human have the capacity to be generous without needing credit, what makes us think that Jesus couldn't or wouldn't operate anonymously? Do we really believe that Jesus won't offer help unless his name is recognized and spoken?

Repeatedly in scripture Jesus heals people and transforms lives in some cases when they don't ask for it, let alone even know who he is. In an earlier chapter we explored the record of the blind man who Jesus healed by spreading mud on his eyes. At the heart of that story was the initiative Jesus took. That blind man didn't know the name of Jesus, didn't believe in Jesus, and didn't even ask for help, but help came nonetheless.

This is what that famous "Footprints" poem is all about. A man has a dream in which he's walking on the beach with Jesus and turns around to see two sets of footprints in the sand. All the while he sees scenes from his life flash across the sky. He notices that during the most difficult times in his life there is only one set of footprints. Discouraged, he says, "Jesus, how come you left me during those times?" Jesus responds, "Those are my footprints: during those tough times, even while you did not recognize me, or call me by name, I was with you. Not only was I with you, I carried you." The feet in that poem are not labeled; anonymous feet and anonymous hands carry us.

This is true grace. It is the kind of grace that we don't have to become Christians for Jesus to pour his grace upon us. At one time or another we have all been the recipients of an anonymous gift. Committing to a Christian path or tradition is a very powerful way to deepen, grow, and connect to the things that matter most. But the Bible does not indicate joining a religion as a prerequisite for getting the help Jesus offers. We do better to be attentive to where God is at work, even when the words, symbols, and context don't seem "Christian."

This is what Paul did. In Acts 17, we learn that Paul visits the Aeropagus, a temple in Athens. In this temple he notices statues devoted to all of their gods. One statue is devoted to an "unknown" god. This is the catch-all statue. The Athenians want to make sure no god is left out. So they essentially say, "To any other god we missed, we honor you too." Surrounded by blasphemous idolatry, the passage tells us Paul is very disturbed by what he sees. But instead of issuing a condemnation of the distractions and atrocities, he does something remarkable.

Paul affirms their religious nature and honors the truth of the unknown god. He then goes on to introduce the name of that God. In so doing, he acknowledges the activity of Jesus in the lives of people who don't know his name. He introduces the name, as if revealing the identity of the anonymous donor already giving to them.

One of the most powerful and difficult things for religious people to do is cross boundaries and see God beyond where he is "supposed" to be. To find God active and alive in what is not sanctioned by religion. This is where Jesus operates repeatedly.

The more we learn to perceive the subtle ways God offers blessings beyond religious boundaries, the more we will experience the Living Water flowing in places we never imagined possible.

25,550 DAYS

An Urgent Invitation

Everyone knew the end was near. As the on-call chaplain in the hospital I was called in to be with the family. Joan was unconscious, but she was still breathing with the help of a machine. The cancer had taken over nearly everything by now. The doctors had done all they could and were about to take her off life support.

The entire family was there except for her eldest son. He had been estranged from his parents for years. Steven had struggled on and off with a serious drug addiction. Eventually, he made it to the bedside of his dying mother. I could tell this was the last place he wanted to be. He was depleted and fragile, but he was there. It was a brave thing to do for someone in his circumstances.

After spending some time with the whole family, I made sure everyone who wanted to was given a chance to say their good-byes to Joan in private. Afterward, we gathered around her bed and I asked her husband to place his hand on Joan's chest so he could feel it rise and fall.

He asked me to pray. Knowing she had been declared brain dead by the doctors, I asked him what he wanted me to pray for. "Healing...that she'll get better," he said. I thought to myself *This guy is in denial.* Still, I did as he asked. I had never been in his shoes before. I trusted he needed this. Then a surprising thing happened. Almost immediately after I prayed for her healing, he said, "You know, it's okay, we can pray that God take her now. I don't want her to suffer." I was stunned by his courage and the speed of acceptance. There is no rulebook for moments like this. Everyone has their own path through grief and loss.

He turned to regard his wife and said, "Joanie, we love you. It's okay for you to go, we will miss you, but we will be okay." Then we prayed for a bit and sat in silence. Not long after this Joan exhaled gently but her chest did not rise again.

I have had the rare privilege to be in this situation more than once, to witness firsthand the last moments of a life. In those final moments, everything in existence comes into the clearest focus. Every time, without fail, I walk away changed. One minute you are with a person you love, the next you are with an arrangement of dust that looks like a bizarre replica of the person you once knew. Inevitable, unavoidable, and it's headed our way.

I followed up with the family a few weeks later when I did the memorial service for Joan, and talked with Steven, her son, again. He was different. I learned that being at his mother's bedside while she died was the hardest thing he had ever done, but he wouldn't trade it for the world. It changed him. He began to realize he was wasting his life. He and his father actually reconciled, recognizing what was important and letting go of what didn't matter. Steven started taking steps to recover from his drug addiction.

Death is a great teacher. It shows us the value of life. Each time we are reminded of the reality of death, it tends to clarify things for us. It has a way of adjusting our priorities and helping us appreciate the gift of life.

This is unique to humans. We are the only species on the planet conscious of the fact that we are currently alive and that one day, we won't be. We have absolutely no idea when we will die. We didn't get an expiration date stamped on our foot.

We may not know when we will die, but we know life doesn't go on in this body forever. If all goes well, and we get to die a "natural" death, we do have an estimate.

25,550.

That's it. Some will get more. Others will get less. But if you live for seventy years that translates into 25,550 days.

If someone gave me that amount of money, I'd be pretty grateful. I could use that to buy an above-average car, or possibly put a down payment on a small home. It might pay for one year of private college education for my kids. But if that's all the money I would ever get in life, it's not much. And, many of those days are gone already and they don't come back.

We are aware that we will die, but generally we don't like to be reminded of it. If we look seriously at death, it is usually followed by a most helpful defense mechanism called denial. We prefer the warm blanket of denial to the icy touch of existential dread. Bear with me, though, for this isn't as depressing as it seems.

Much of life is lived as an immortality project. Behind most things we do, death is an unconscious driver. We do all kinds of things to try and conquer the inconvenient reality of our mortality. We get married and have children so that they will carry on some part of us. We build skyscrapers, statues, businesses, and strip malls so that something will endure after we are gone. Some are deluded enough to write books in an unconscious effort to ensure their thoughts will remain after they die.

The immortality project is simply this: There must be a way, somehow, that we can conquer death. The strange thing is, deep down we know all things eventually return to dust. Some just last a little longer than others.

This awareness is what drives fundamental human questions. Who am I? Why am I here? Is this all there is? What happens when it's all over? The human conundrum is to exist and to wonder why. To breathe and know it's coming to an end.

This condition and questioning has given birth to the major religions. Each one promises to solve the crisis of meaning and the problem of death.

The most common solution offered by Christianity is that Jesus conquered death. If we place our trust in him, we can conquer death too. If we believe the right things, act the right way, or belong to the right group we will go to heaven when we die. Get it right in this life and our eternal reward is waiting for us in the next life. Get it wrong now and something worse awaits. Either way, for much of religious Christianity, the point of *this* life is to prepare for the *next* life.

Our focus on what happens to us after we die is understandable and probably inevitable. We humans have an innate curiosity about what lies beyond this life. But given our interest in the Christian religion's emphasis on the afterlife, I find it particularly fascinating that Jesus didn't talk much about what happens when we die. This is one of the most pressing questions we have, and yet this master teacher, Son of God, and savior makes only passing mention of it.

Not only that, Jesus got to peek behind the curtain. He actually died. We're talking three days dead. He spent a long weekend in the afterlife and lived to tell the story. People in our culture die for a few minutes on an operating table and go on to write entire bestselling books about the experience. But Jesus? He spent three whole days in that place and when he returned here's what he had to say about it.

Nothing. Nada. Zip.

What did he talk about when he came back after death? Here's just a sampling: He tells his disciples to make students of him (see Matthew

28:16); to share the good news of liberation in *this* life (see Mark 16:9–20). He says, "Peace be with you," and "I'm hungry" (see Luke 24:36–41). He says, "Receive the Holy Breath, now you can forgive sins" (see John 20:22). He says, "It's me, really, touch my side" (see John 20:27) and "The fishing is better on the right side of the boat" (see John 21:6). He says, "Let's eat" (see John 21), "Feed my sheep, now follow me" (see John 21:18–20).

The most striking comment is found in John 21:22. Here Jesus and Peter are talking after his resurrection and Peter wants to know the fate of one of the other disciples. Jesus says, and I'm paraphrasing here, "It's none of your business what happens to him. Your job is to follow me. That's it. So stop worrying about the future fate of other people." It's a stinging rebuke for Peter, and for any of us who have gotten caught up in worrying about the long-term fate of others. Jesus is pretty clear in this verse— what happens later is God's business not ours.

The account of Jesus' words after his resurrection hardly forms a systematic theology of the afterlife. Mostly it's a repeated invitation to trust and follow him and not worry about the future. Apparently, he was also hungry a lot.

If the afterlife was important to him, you'd

think he would have written about it. Or preached a sermon or two. But he didn't. After Jesus rose from the dead, he spent his time directing our attention to this life. That suggests this life matters as much or more to him as the next. And if this life matters to Jesus, perhaps it should matter to us too.

We only get one. And it's short.

I was in a restaurant in another country. I didn't speak the language and couldn't read the menu. In broken English, the waiter tried to explain these strange dishes to my friends and me. He described a six-course meal, everything building to the epic final dish. What I understood sounded delicious, especially the last dish. As he brought out each course I ate small amounts so I could save up for the final dish.

As we got closer I decided to skip one of the dishes that didn't look that interesting to leave room for the last one. After that dish, the waiter cleared the table, and brought the check. I had lost count. I didn't realize that the one dish I had skipped was actually the final one I was waiting for—the one I most wanted to try! What I thought was an appetizer was actually the entrée.

This is what happens when we think salvation is what we get when we die. We separate this life from the next life. We assume that it's all about the next life and this one is merely a prelude. But what if life now is meant to be an entrée, not just an appetizer?

Jesus wanted us to see the gift we've already been given, not just the one we're waiting to enjoy. If we can't understand and appreciate the incredible gift of this life, what on earth makes us think we'll even recognize, let alone appreciate, the next one?

For Jesus, salvation is here and now, as much as it will be there and then. And our recognition of it now seems to matter a lot to him.

THE EYE OF THE HURRICANE

We find the same truth expressed in the Lord's Prayer. Jesus tells us to pray, "Let your will be done *on earth* as it is in heaven." We are to pray for heaven on earth, in this life. When Jesus announces freedom for the oppressed, healing for the sick, food for the hungry, and the call to make peace, this is a vision of heaven on earth. However, his vision is not merely a call to reorder the structures and powers in society. This is not an impersonal and systemic vision of heaven.

The heaven Jesus talked about is not dependent on fixing all the problems of the world. Quite the opposite is true. Speaking to his followers in John 16:33 he says, "I have told you these things, so that in me you may have peace. *In this world you will have trouble*. But take heart! I have overcome the world" (emphasis added). Jesus promises trouble and struggle in life. This is simply the nature of this world. Rather than changing its nature, Jesus offers something better. He has *overcome* the world.

In the midst of the terrors and traumas of life, he promises the possibility of a peace that passes understanding even when things don't go the way we want them. Even in the throes of injustice, betrayal, abuse, and injury, he promises the possibility of a joy-filled life that is immune from the "good" and "bad" things that happen to us. Like learning to live in the eye of a hurricane—all around the storm may rage, but in the center is a place of peace undisturbed.

The salvation or heaven Jesus talked about is for people, not societies, groups, or institutions. An institution can't feel love, peace, or joy. Those are human experiences. Jesus certainly confronted the powers and institutions of his day, but he wasn't trying to save them. He came to save people, most often from themselves.

The good news begins with us as individuals.

Jesus was more than a savior for the next life, or an ethical teacher for social ills. He was a master of the inner life. He knew how to direct and connect his followers to the source of water flowing within that is never diminished or diverted in the face of life's problems.

Some will read this and think such an understanding of salvation is too self-centered, individualistic, or even narcissistic. What about helping others? What about social injustice, war, disease, and starving people?

An answer to these questions might be available if we answer a different set of questions. If there is an endless supply of water, is it selfish to drink it when you're thirsty? Moreover, if you abstain from drinking that water, does that help others quench their thirst?

Another way to say this is: an unlit lamp cannot light another lamp. If we want to bring light into a room, we must light the wick of our lamp. If we want world peace, we must begin by finding peace in our own lives. Otherwise we are the blind leading the blind.

When we experience kindness, grace, and

gratitude on the inside, it finds a way outside. The opposite is also true. The war that rages on the inside is the source of countless wars on the outside. Whether it's a war between spouses, tribes, or nations. As long as we are convinced that peace can only be found by rearranging everything outside of us, we will be perpetually disappointed. That's like trying to manage and organize waves on the surface of the ocean. It is their nature to change. Every time we solve one problem, a new one pops up like an interminable game of whack-a-mole.

We should not neglect issues of justice and peace in the world. These are noble and important causes, worthy of our best efforts. However, we must be careful not to neglect the world within us or both will suffer.

This is the aspect of the good news that seems most often overlooked or ignored. The salvation or heaven we long for is *within us now*. And finding it in this life now matters a lot to Jesus.

WHILE THE SUN STILL SHINES

The other day I went into my garage in the middle of the day and flipped the switch to turn on the light. No light came on. The bulb was burned out. But there was enough light from the windows that I could still see what I was doing. I did what I needed to do and went back in the house. Later that night I needed something from the garage again. So I went out, flipped the switch, and nothing happened. I couldn't see a thing. And my flashlight was conveniently packed away in my camping gear, also in the garage. I probably should have fixed the bulb when it was still light out. Because when the darkness came, I was stuck.

For Jesus, our lives are lived during the daylight hours. As long as we are breathing, the sun is out even though it is heading for the great horizon. Eventually the sun will set and the night will come. That is the nature of our existence—it's a gift that comes to an end. Jesus wants us to know about another source of light, one that has no relationship to this fading sun, one that burns before the sun rises and persists long after the sun sets. Jesus wants us to turn that light on now, not wait until it is too dark to see. The light Jesus talks about is *the* Light, eternal life, heaven itself. And he returns us to this message again and again. There is an urgency to his message. He knows the importance of finding that light while the sun is still out, because when the sun sets and the darkness comes, it's difficult to find much of anything.

Find the heaven now, and it is ours for eternity.

DOLLS OF DIRT

The Forgotten Miracle

The two blue tackling dummies were arranged on the ground in parallel form, creating an artificial lane between them. I stood in the gap assuming a well-intentioned but timid sumo stance. On this occasion, the starting middle linebacker and also the captain of the high school football team played the role of ball carrier. My job was to practice my tackling form as he ran through the hole. It was supposed to be a half-speed drill, but Travis was coming in full throttle.

Even as a junior in high school, he was a neck-less, 215-pound wrecking ball of a kid who could bench press nearly twice his body weight. As a sophomore, and third-string linebacker, I was a doughy 170 pounds with the competitive drive of a hamster. It was an epic showdown between a docile furry creature and a mass of muscle with some serious momentum.

Thankfully, the moment between the point of contact and me splayed flat on my back, I don't recall. What I know is that my body covered an impressive distance both in terms of height and length. I laid

on the ground gasping for air and nothing was happening. A panic set in as it occurred to me I might
not make it. Then suddenly a huge breath returned,
filled my lungs, and saved my life.

Getting the wind knocked out of you is a
strange experience. It is so completely harmless and
yet few things rival the panic it can induce when
you experience it. The phrase "getting the wind
knocked out of you" hardly does justice to the experience. Perhaps a more fitting term is a *near-death
experience*.

Nothing quite shows us the importance of our
breath like its temporary departure.

In Genesis there is an account of God creating the first human. It says, "And the Lord God
formed Adam from the dust of the ground and
breathed into the nostrils the breath of life and
Adam became alive" (2:7). The Old Testament was
originally written in Hebrew, and layers of meaning
in the original language don't show up as clearly in
English.

Two very important and simple truths about
the nature of existence are revealed in this verse.

First, the English word "Adam" is the Hebrew word "*ha-adam*," which comes from the root word "*ha-adama*" meaning *ground* or *earth*. Here "adam" is not used as a proper name, but rather a Hebrew noun that describes the physical makeup of a human being. The writer is making an explicit connection between the "earthling" and the earth that it came from.

Second, the English word "breath" in this passage is the Hebrew word "*neshamah*," which also means *soul* or *spirit*. In English, the concepts of breath and spirit are usually regarded as two separate things. One is physical; the other is philosophical or religious. One is a physiological mechanism that delivers oxygen to organs, the other is an immaterial belief in an animating invisible force. But to the Hebrew imagination, these two are one. They use the same word to describe something we see as two separate things. For the Hebrews, the breath is not a metaphor of Spirit. The breath is Spirit.

The breath you just took is no less than the infinite creative force of the universe filling your body. Hidden inside every breath is the river of life Jesus promises. We can no more be separated from this river than we can our breath. It dances and flows within us.

Another way to translate this verse then is

"God formed a doll of dirt from the dust of the earth, breathed Divine Spirit into the nostrils and made it live." The perpetual motion of inhale and exhale is the most important gift we've been given. It constitutes the fundamental mystery and beauty of our existence. Its first arrival is how we determine a child lives, and its final departure is the way we determine one's death. Between the first inhale and the last exhale is life. Every single breath contains the gift of *zoe*. We don't even have to think about it to receive it. We don't even have to believe in it for that matter and it still comes. But if we remain unconscious, we will miss it.

This story is a poetic description of a simple observation of reality. As humans, we are comprised of the same chemical composition as dirt. Carbon, hydrogen, oxygen, water, calcium, and trace amounts of a dozen or more minerals. What that means is when we take a shower, we are merely dirt washing off dirt.

While I'm made of dirt, one key difference exists between the dirt and me. One thing separates me from being treated like dirt. And that is the breath I just took. When the breath comes, I am dirt that laughs, cries, loves, hates, fears, tastes, touches, writes, dances, thinks, doubts, believes, and more. And as long as the breath continues to come, all of this is possible for me.

When we forget this, we become incredibly arrogant dirt. We become like the leaf blown by the wind that suddenly thinks it can fly. When the wind subsides, the leaf returns to the ground. We would do well to remember we are like that leaf, capable of nothing without the courtesy of the breath, *neshamah*, Spirit, *zoe*.

When the breath stops, we return to the earth. We cease being human and are once again dirt— no more, no less. We will be treated accordingly, placed in a container surrounded by our fellow dirt. That's when the party stops. Even our loved ones won't want us around anymore. Dirt that has breath really doesn't like spending time with formerly breathing dirt. It reminds us this life comes to an end. On the whole, we really like the breath staying in us as long as possible. Something in us knows how precious this gift really is. One day most of us will have a chance to become conscious of what it is. The day we realize we are very near the end, when only a few breaths remain, that is when we will see it for what it is. But we don't have to wait until then. The river is meant to be enjoyed now.

If we want to find the river, it is flowing just beneath our noses. Jesus came to make the introduction. When we understand the breath, we will understand grace. The breath is the ultimate blessing, the true grace. Breath accepts being slighted, rejected, and ignored. It doesn't judge or seek attention. It is as subtle as a drop of water and as powerful as a river that carves canyons from stone.

It does not withhold itself based on what we believe or don't believe, what we have done or have left undone. It is faithful even when everything and everyone else around us fails. When other people say they don't love us anymore, or even hate us. The breath never agrees with them. It is the only thing in existence that stays with us till the very end. No intermediary exists between our breath and us. Nothing stands in the way of this incredible river and nothing needs to.

"Grace," "God," "Love," "*zoe*," and "breath" are merely different words we use in an attempt to name the same reality.

The breath precedes religion, doctrine, and dogma. It is the great Guest to whom we play temporary host. It is the Living Water that existed long before merchants like religion came along, set up shop, gave it a name, and created barriers and divisions. Most of the time we are oblivious to this fact.

We are like a fish in the river searching desperately for the very water that flows through us and in us. This is both funny and tragic. But here is what separates us from all other creatures that breathe. We can actually become conscious of the gift and learn to recognize the miracle of this existence. When we do, when the connection is made, something beautiful happens. You've heard the saying "empty-handed we came and empty-handed we go." Well, if we drink from this river while we live, we may enter this life empty-handed but we don't have to leave that way.

THE GIFT ALREADY GIVEN

I looked in the small gray cardboard box one more time, then closed the lid and put it in the glove compartment of my car. I was just out of college, a few months into my first job, and jittery as I drove in to work. The box was sent to me by a woman who would become my grandmother-in-law. We already had the kind of relationship that made the phrase "in-law" feel too detached. The fact that she entrusted me with this particular gift was further evidence of my full adoption as her grandson.

As I drove, one thought jackhammered through my head—*Don't lose this. Don't lose this. Don't lose this. Whatever you do, DO NOT LOSE THIS.* I parked the car in the ramp outside the office, turned off the ignition, and paused to contemplate my options. *I'm going to leave it in the car, that way I won't lose it.* Then an even more paranoid thought crossed my mind, *What if the car gets stolen?!* I couldn't risk it. The matter was settled, I would carry the box with me all day until I could deliver it later that evening.

I took the box out and placed it in my front pocket. My hand rested nervously on the visible and awkward lump it created. I got out of the car, started walking, and was gripped by a temporary bout of obsessive-compulsive disorder. It compelled me to check the box just one more time to ensure the contents were still present and accounted for. I pulled the box out of my pocket, opened the lid slowly, and peered inside.

In that moment, my worst fear unfolded before me like a predator's wings. I couldn't believe my eyes. The box was empty. It was gone. I frantically searched the ground around me, fished through all my pockets, gave myself a police pat down, then rushed back to inspect the glove box of the car—nothing.

Next was shock. With the car door still ajar and alarm gently binging, I walked off toward the office in a cool haze of denial. Within a few steps I regressed to the solutions of a four-year-old and thought *Call Mom, she will fix it.* This was a perfectly understandable regression when you consider the gravity of what I had just lost.

Inside this box was a diamond. Not just any diamond. This one was almost a karat in size with impeccable clarity, cut, and color. The gem was appraised at roughly six months of my salary at the time, way beyond anything I could have afforded. But this was the least of its value. Its true worth could not be reduced to a number. This precious stone was a gift given to my grandmother-in-law by her husband who had passed away nearly fifteen years before.

She kept it all these years and had entrusted it to me after I asked for her granddaughter's hand in marriage. She said if I wanted, I could use it for an engagement ring. I humbly and happily accepted and assured her it would be in good hands. I had an appointment at a jeweler to have the diamond set later that night. And somewhere between my home and the parking ramp, I lost it.

Upon returning from the ludicrous fantasy that

my mom could do anything about this problem, I gathered my wits, went back to the car, and started searching again. I looked under the car, I triple- and quadruple-checked the glove box and my pockets but found nothing. Then, feeling a bit desperate after more fruitless searching, I decided to get creative. I checked under the driver seat for no apparent reason.

There in the darkness under the seat I noticed a small round shadow. I reached in, felt around until I hit upon a small hard object with my fingers, and pulled it out to see the priceless stone sparkling like it was winking at me. It had fallen out of the box as the box passed over the center console, slipped between the seats, and bounced underneath—an improbable fluke of the worst kind. But now what was lost was found and all was well in the world. The rest of the day, my hand never left the pocket the diamond was in. I knew where it was at all times.

During this episode something interesting happened. As long as the diamond was in the box, the box was as precious as the stone it held. The box never became a diamond, but it borrowed the value of it. As long as I knew the diamond was inside it, I treated it with the greatest care. However, the moment I realized the box no longer held the diamond, the box lost all value. I don't even know what happened to it. My only interest was the diamond.

As long as we are alive, we are like that box with a diamond inside. Our body is the box, and our breath, the Divine, is the diamond. As long as the diamond is in the box, the box is worth more than we can imagine.

One day the diamond will be removed from the box, and the box will be thrown aside. If we can understand the hidden value of what's inside, we will get to enjoy it now and long after the box is discarded. If we fail to understand what the box contains, we will treat it haphazardly and fail to recognize how rich we really are. And when the box is thrown away, we won't realize a diamond has gone with it.

Jesus came to show us the incredible truth that while we are alive, we are the carriers of a price-less diamond. Speaking to his disciples he says, "On that day you will realize that I am in my Father, and you are in me, and I am in you" (John 14:20). There will come a day when we will realize what has been true all along. We will recognize the real-ity that we are God carriers, where the Infinite has come to live in the finite for a limited time.

Jesus did not come to start a new religion or

a new social order. He didn't come that we would become more religious or even more spiritual. Jesus came to show us what it truly means to be *human*— to live life conscious of the exquisite gift we've been given. He came to introduce us to the most easily forgotten and often overlooked miracle of all—our existence and the heaven hidden within it.

GRATITUDES

This book is a product of years of reflection, listening, study, teaching, conversation, and practice. Many people had a hand in its creation. Some were involved indirectly, others were faithful readers of the manuscript and offered critical feedback on my prose, logic, language, imagery, and pacing. I am deeply grateful to the following people for their support, challenge, participation, and friendship.

I want to thank Bahar Anooshahr, Rob Bell, Nadia Bolz-Weber, Tony Jones, Brian McLaren, and Mike Volkema for their honest, insightful, and invaluable feedback on the early drafts of this manuscript. To Brad, my brother, a supremely gifted writer, for his relentless capacity to see gaps in logic, offer lessons in syntax, and support me in this work. To my mom and dad for their endless enthusiasm, attention to detail, and well...life.

To Chris Ferebee, my agent, for his persistent generosity, advocacy, and friendship.

To Wendy Grisham, my publisher, for believing in the content of this book.

To Adrienne Ingrum, my editor, for discerning the identity of this book and calling it forth with authority and grace.

To Jim McNeish, for the generous space he offered to reflect, breathe, and grow.

To Prem Rawat, for his clarity, wisdom, and insight about this life.

To Andrea, for all her direct and indirect support. But especially for the selfless care of our children during the many hours I was absent in writing land.

And last but not least, I want to express my appreciation to Mars Hill Bible Church and Trinity Mennonite Church. You have given me the incredible honor of time, attention, and trust as a teacher. You are rare communities of faith who model what it means to remove the barriers on our way to finding the river.

ABOUT THE AUTHOR

SHANE HIPPS is a sought-after speaker and teaching pastor at Mars Hill Bible Church in Grand Rapids, Michigan, where he shared the stage with Rob Bell. Previously he served for five years as the Lead Pastor of Trinity Mennonite Church in Phoenix, Arizona. He is a graduate of Fuller Seminary, the result of a self-termed "Damascus" experience. Before accepting his call as a pastor, he was a strategic planner in advertising for the multimillion-dollar communications plan for Porsche. Shane is author of the award-winning book *Flickering Pixels: How Technology Shapes Your Faith*, and *The Hidden Power of Electronic Culture: How Media Shapes Faith, The Gospel, and Church*.

In 2011, Shane launched three films of talks he gave on the topics of technology and faith, preaching, and human development. These are available for download on his website, which also features over three hundred sortable teachings. In 2012, he was featured in the Animate film series produced by Sparkhouse. Shane is also the founder of Lantern, Inc., a leadership development and consulting company. Learn more at www.shanehipps.com or follow him on Twitter @shanehipps.

ADDITIONAL COPYRIGHT INFORMATION